LOVING YOUR STEPFAMILY

Single Parents / Blending Families
—Nuclear Bonds—

LOVING YOUR STEPFAMILY

The Art of Making Your Blending Family Work

Dr. Donald R. Partridge
Jenetha Partridge

Pleasanton, California

LOVING YOUR STEPFAMILY:
THE ART OF MAKING YOUR BLENDING FAMILY WORK
Authors: Dr. Donald R. Partridge / Jenetha Partridge

 Institute for Family Research and Education (IFRE)
P.O. Box 10092
Pleasanton, CA 94588-0092 U.S.A.

Phone: 925-351-7000
E-Mail: info@blendingfamily.com
Web: http://www.blendingfamily.com

Copyright © 2007 Donald R. Partridge

ISBN-13 978-0-9795110-0-4

Publisher's Cataloging-in-Publication Data

Partridge, Donald Roudi.
    Loving your stepfamily : the art of making your blending family work / Donald R. Partridge, Jenetha Partridge.

    p. cm.
    Includes index.

    ISBN 978-0-9795110-0-4

1. Stepfamilies—United States. 2. Stepparents—United States. 3. Stepchildren—United States. 4. Remarriage—United States. 5. Family life. 6. Family—Religious aspects—Christianity. I. Partridge, Jenetha. II. Title.

HQ777.7 P

646.7819—dc22   2007926501

Printed and bound in the United States of America.

The silhouette logo and some other images in this publication were designed by Christopher Blunden of PresentationLab.com from Lotus SmartPics © 1991 Lotus Development Corporation.

Scripture references are taken from the New King James Version of the Bible. Copyright © 1982 by Thomas Nelson, Inc. Used by permission. All rights reserved.

Interior design by One-On-One Book Production, West Hills, California.
Cover design by Renae Forrey.

Here's What People Are Saying about
Loving Your Stepfamily

In examining Dr. Partridge's materials, I have been struck by the wisdom of his ideas, couched in an entirely unique vocabulary. The proof that his principles work can be witnessed in his own thriving stepfamily and the testimonials of the hundreds of families he has helped find peace and stability. – William T. Follette, M.D., Chief of Psychiatry (Ret.), Kaiser Permanente – San Francisco, CA

In my 25 years of ministry, I have not known anyone who is more uniquely qualified to address the complexities of the modern family. Dr. Don Partridge is not afraid to deal directly with the messy challenges of blended family dynamics and provides a practical road map toward healthy relationships in the family system. – Dr. John Merritt, Senior Pastor, CrossWinds Church – Dublin, CA

Donald Partridge knows first-hand the many varied and complex challenges of blending families. His material is forthright, illuminating, thought-provoking, targeted, and extremely pragmatic—he truly helps single parents identify and find solutions for the countless issues they face when merging their families. Highly recommended reading! – Dennis Franck, Director, Single Adult Ministries, General Council of the Assemblies of God – Springfield, MO

Dr. Partridge is the expert we need in our churches to deal with the complexities of single parents and stepfamilies. His teaching and programs are invaluable. – Don Reed, Executive Minister, Northern California Baptist Conference – Tracy, CA

In the area of family ministry, few understand the issues as well. – Dr. Sam J. Earp, Executive Pastor, Calvary Church – Los Gatos, CA

In 14 years as a single parent, I have read it all and heard it all. There is nothing existing today that deals with the complexities of such a dynamic environment as Dr. Partridge's materials. Finally, a fresh new approach that truly understands these issues. – Reviewer, Community Presbyterian Church – Danville, CA

We walked into our second and third marriage thinking we knew what to do. Now with Dr. Partridge's book, we do. – Reviewer, Woodmen Valley Church – Colorado Springs, CO

I would give all I own if the divorce process required both parents to hear Dr. Partridge's information. The deepest agony of my life was powerlessly watching my ex excoriate me to our 4-yr-old, making a tender happy child confused and miserable for the better part of a decade. – Reviewer, Calvary Church – Los Gatos, CA

I've been in singles ministry for twenty years and I've never heard this before. It's incredible! – Reviewer, Cathedral of Faith – San Jose, CA

I would have given anything to have had this information available five years ago when I met my husband. I am certain the pain and difficulties we are experiencing could have been avoided. Thank God for this material. – Reviewer, Calvary Church – Los Gatos, CA

Dedication

This book is dedicated to:

all adults in stepfamilies,
all single parents who will date and remarry,
all adults without children who will marry
adults with children.

We know your hopes and struggles…
We've been where you are right now…
You will find real-life answers in this book.

Acknowledgments

We are deeply indebted to Jenetha's father, Attorney Stuart S. Rough, for his tremendous encouragement and support, and to Don's mother, Dr. Elizabeth Glenn, for her endless hours of commentary and editing.

Words cannot express our gratitude to Clyde and Sue Brewster, companions and colleagues and friends, who have given so much of themselves to us and to our work for single parents and blending families. Thanks to Christopher Blunden, J.D., who has served this work so faithfully with his wisdom and friendship.

We also want to acknowledge and thank our seven wonderful children: Elizabeth Alcamo; Lesley Livingston; 1stLt Matthew Weaver, USMC; 2ndLt Dustin Partridge, USMC; Devon Weaver; Krissa Partridge; and Pfc. Christopher Partridge, USMC, who faithfully hung in there during our sacrifices to make this book a reality.

Last, no acknowledgments would be complete without thanking Dr. Hollis Green, Th.D., Ph.D., Chancellor of *Oxford Graduate School: American Centre for Religion & Society Studies (ACRSS)* for his encouragement, belief, and challenge that one individual can make a difference for Christ in our society and world.

Disclaimer

Although the authors and publisher have made every effort to insure the accuracy and completeness of information contained in this book, they assume no responsibility for errors, inaccuracies, omissions, or inconsistencies. Any slights of people, places, or organizations are unintentional. Readers should use their own judgment or consult a professional counselor for specific solutions to personal problems.

Contents

PREFACE   **xi**

INTRODUCTION: STEPFAMILIES ARE NOTHING
LIKE FIRST MARRIAGES
Another Universe   **1**

PRINCIPLE 1: UNDERSTAND

1. THE MOST POWERFUL BONDS IN THE WORLD—
   THE BONDS BETWEEN HUSBAND AND WIFE
   AND PARENT AND CHILD
   Nuclear Bonds   **11**

2. WHY MERGING TWO FAMILIES SO OFTEN FAILS
   The Problem with Joining Nuclear Bonds   **18**

PRINCIPLE 2: IDENTIFY

3. IDENTIFYING THE CRITICAL RELATIONSHIPS
   IN YOUR NEW FAMILY
   Identifying All Bonds and Connections   **27**

PRINCIPLE 3: ACCEPT

4. ACCEPTING YOUR CHILDREN'S OTHER PARENT
   INTO THEIR LIVES
   Accepting All Outside Bonds and Connections   **39**

5. ACCEPTING YOUR SPOUSE'S CHILDREN
   INTO YOUR LIFE
   Accepting All Inside Connections   **49**

6. THE TRUE ROLE OF THE STEPPARENT
   Accepting the Stepparent as a Stepparent   **58**

7. THE AUTHORITY OF THE BIOLOGICAL PARENT
   IN DISCIPLINE
   Accepting the Discipline Process   **68**

PRINCIPLE 4: SEPARATE

8. LETTING YOUR EX LIVE HIS (HER) OWN LIFE
   Separating from All Outside Bonds and Connections   87

9. GIVING FREEDOM TO THE PARENT/CHILD
   RELATIONSHIP
   On Occasion, Separating from Inside Connections   96

PRINCIPLE 5: BENEFIT

10. *MAKING* PEACE WITH YOUR EX AND YOUR
    EX'S PARTNER
    Benefiting All Outside Bonds and Connections   107

11. GOING THE DISTANCE WITH YOUR STEPCHILDREN
    Benefiting All Inside Connections   119

12. ALLOWING CHILDREN ALONE TIME WITH
    THEIR OWN PARENT
    Benefiting Inside Bonds Through Individual Attention   127

13. MAKING EVERY FAMILY MEMBER FEEL VALUED
    Zero Neglect Toward Any Bond or Connection   134

14. LOVING YOUR STEPFAMILY
    What Grace and Forgiveness Really Look Like   143

APPENDIX

END-NOTES   151
A GUIDE FOR GROUP STUDY:
  Questions for Thought and Discussion   156

INDEX   165
ABOUT THE AUTHORS   169

Preface

You have in your hands timeless principles that will give you clear direction on how to build a great stepfamily. Your stepfamily will thrive or fail depending on how well you incorporate them into your daily lives.

The solutions shared in this book have helped hundreds of families build great stepfamilies. They have also helped our own stepfamily become great, too—a stepfamily now over twenty years in the making.

These principles are so vitally important that you will find yourself using them throughout the life of your stepfamily. As the years pass, they will be to you a strong and steady guide. Your family will continue to transform and find more and more stability as these principles continue to work. We consistently have people write to us years later saying, "They're still working!"

Are these principles easy to learn? Yes, very easy to learn, and very easy to remember.

Are these principles well known? Surprisingly, no! Most couples are taken aback when they first hear about them and tell us that they've never heard them before.

Are these principles that important? Vitally important. Statistics say that between 65 and 70 percent of stepfamilies fail.[1] This means that something is terribly wrong, especially in a society such as ours, one of the most enlightened and educated on the planet. What is wrong is lack of understanding of the stepfamily system and lack of the knowledge and skills to make it work.

The principles outlined in this book are the foundation for making your stepfamily successful. Committing to and faithfully utilizing them will solve most of the problems common to every stepfamily. We call them high-speed solutions because when they are understood and acted on, you will find immediate positive changes.

The art of making your blending family work is to learn and understand these basic concepts and to incorporate them into your every action and word. Success will come when they have permeated your every decision and behavior.

May God bless you and your blending family as you discover the simple, transforming, and timeless principles in Loving Your Stepfamily.

Donald Partridge
Jenetha Partridge

Pleasanton, California

INTRODUCTION:
Stepfamilies Are Nothing Like First Marriages
Another Universe

Below are two families: the husband and wife on the left are in a first marriage; the husband and wife on the right are in what we call a blending family, or a stepfamily.

First Family   Blending Family

Figure I

Both families appear identical. Just looking at them you would probably say that the two families seem to be quite similar.

But other than what you see in the illustration—man, woman, kids—they are not the slightest bit alike. They are as different as you can get. It's like comparing a fish with a bird, a rock with water, life on the planet Earth with life in outer space.

You might say, "Wait a minute, what do you mean they are as different as life on planet Earth and life in outer space?"

This is our point. Stepfamilies live in another universe.

Myth: We can apply the rules in a first marriage to a blending family

Stepfamilies live in deep space, in a world entirely different from that of a first-marriage family. The common myth is that stepfamilies are basically like first-marriage families, that all families operate by the same principles and rules. It is this myth that is so destructive to the blending family. And believing this myth is what contributes to the high number of divorces and causes blending families to experience constant difficulties.

> *The laws and rules and principles that work for first marriages in the first universe on planet Earth don't apply to blending families. Blending families live in another universe under an entirely different set of rules and principles that have nothing to do with first marriages and nothing to do with what is known and what is familiar.*

Life in the first universe consists of childhood, adolescence, dating, and marriage—standard stages and transitions of life. We understand these stages; the rules are clear. Bookshelves are filled with information about common, normal life transitions.

But when you have children and then divorce, you are thrown into a new universe, into deep space, into an environment that is completely unfamiliar and unknown. You enter this new universe without preparation and without knowledge and are forced to learn as you go, by trial and error—usually with more error than anything else. Being a single parent or living in a blending family is not part of the normal stages of life.

Deep space is all about ex-spouses, ex-relatives, children moving back and forth between households, about caring for a family alone, about not being with your children when you want to. Dating a parent in the new universe is not about dating a single individual, it's about dating a crowd—you date the parent, the child, the relatives of that child, the other parent, the other parent's new partner, and on and on. And when you remarry, it's about another partner with completely new rules and traditions, living with non-biological family members, stepparent/stepchildren relationships, and far less control.

Apply the rules of a first marriage to this other universe and catastrophe will occur. Laws on planet Earth don't apply to families in deep space. They will ruin a good family. Living in another universe means living by new principles completely different from anything you have previously encountered.

Home Depot: Can't I just go to the store?

Let's compare a first marriage family with a blending family. Suppose the first-marriage dad is going off to purchase some lumber to repair the back fence on a Saturday morning. The dad and his wife have two kids, Larry, age twelve and Billy, age ten. Here is a typical Saturday morning conversation:

Husband: *"I'm taking Larry to Home Depot; we'll be back soon."*
Wife: *"What are you going to buy?"*
Husband: *"Some lumber to repair the fence."*
Wife: *"Okay. See you in a little while."*

That's it! That's how things go in a first marriage! The first-marriage family has no difficulty with dad going off to Home Depot with one of his sons. Larry's ready to go, Billy's fine if he goes or stays, and mom is comfortable with the whole thing. Life is simple on planet Earth.

Now, let's look at the same situation in a blending family. This time, Larry is the husband's biological son; Billy is the wife's biological son. Let's see what happens:

Husband: *"I'm taking Larry to Home Depot; we'll be back soon."*
Wife, feeling hurt, thinks: *"Why doesn't he take my son, too?"*
Billy sadly thinks: *"I wish I could go. He never invites me."*
Larry, reacting with happiness, thinks: *"Oh, boy, time alone just with my dad!"*
Husband, noticing the negative reactions, thinks: *"Can't I do anything with just my own son?"*

The husband learns quickly that he has made a mistake by not inviting Billy. The next Saturday, he's determined to make things right.

Husband: *"I'm taking Larry AND Billy to Home Depot; we'll be back soon."*

Wife, feeling hurt, thinks: *"Why does he spend all his time with the kids and not me?"*

Billy, a little bummed, thinks: *"Larry always gets the front seat when his dad drives. And the only reason my stepdad is inviting me is because he thinks he has to."*

Larry, somewhat depressed, thinks: *"Why can't I spend time with my dad without always having to drag Billy along?"*

Husband, seeing everyone's negative reaction, thinks: *"Can't I just go to Home Depot without a family meltdown?"*

The dad couldn't understand why everyone in his family was so sensitive. The dad was expecting everyone to respond like family members in a first marriage—just not possible in the new universe. Dad and mom needed to go through deep space training. Because they didn't know how to manage a family in the second universe, the entire family had negative reactions to a very simple event.

You might now think that the problem is the second universe, that it must be a miserable place to live. But the problem isn't the second universe. The problem is lack of understanding and lack of preparation for the second universe.

The second universe is actually a great place to live. Preparation and following the rules are the keys to success.

Myth: We'll soon be back on planet Earth

Some people in blending families may think to themselves, "Okay, I'm convinced we're in another universe. I see it all around me. But we're not going to be here long. We'll eventually get back to planet Earth."

Not true! You will never be like a first-marriage family. You will never operate by the same rules. The internal operations of a blending family will always require adherence to the rules and principles of deep space. Any time parents begin to believe that their blending family is now like a first-marriage family and start to think like a first-marriage family, their blending family will immediately begin to disintegrate.

Single parents, dating parents, and blending couples may as well begin to learn the rules and principles of the second universe because they are in it for life. Live by the proper principles, and things will go well for you. Ignore the rules, and deep space can become a terribly miserable experience.

Answers and solutions!

If you know the rules and principles and follow them, the second universe can be extremely satisfying. You don't have to return to planet Earth or try to live like somebody in a first marriage to feel happy and fulfilled. Life in your blending family can work and can be wonderful. Your blending family can be freed from constant problems. Trips to the Home Depot on Saturday can go smoothly. Your stepparent and stepchildren connections can improve significantly. Even contacts with your ex-spouses can become highly manageable. The reality is that your blending family can and should operate reasonably well.

The second universe is not one of chaos and complexity beyond your capabilities. It can become knowable and workable. Why do we know this? Because the Bible says *God created the heavens and the earth*.[1] God not only created planet Earth but the heavens too—meaning He created ALL things, including the universe of the stepfamily. He knows and understands its laws and principles because He created them. The very fact that all things are created by God means that everything is designed to work well and run smoothly. Stepfamilies are designed to be peaceful and satisfying.

Can your family find peace and happiness? Of course! Can your children come out of your blending family stable and emotionally healthy? Yes!

When Jenetha and I blended our family, we, too, were thrown into the second universe, into deep space, and nothing seemed to work. Once we learned the key principles of the new universe and mastered the necessary skills, we experienced happiness and closeness that would rival those in any first marriage.

The good news is that through God's help and wisdom *your* family can be a great family, too! But it requires throwing out familiar ways of doing things and getting used to new tools, new thinking, and new behaviors.

---~⁓---

Making Your Blending Family Work

Through wisdom a house is built, and understanding is established, by knowledge the rooms are filled with all precious and pleasant riches.

Proverbs 24:3-4

Principle 1

UNDERSTAND

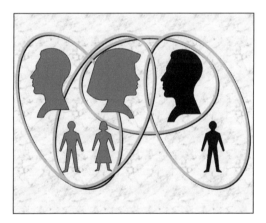

1

THE MOST POWERFUL BONDS IN THE WORLD:
The Bonds Between Husband And Wife And Parent And Child
Nuclear Bonds

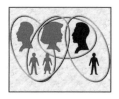

A first marriage with children is a *simple* family system, with everyone sharing the same biological bond. A blending family is a *complex* family system consisting of biological and non-biological relationships.

Accompanying these complex relationships, unfortunately, are common myths and misunderstandings that can completely dismantle your family. The lack of understanding of these relationships will plague your family with ongoing difficulties.

The first-marriage bond

When couples marry, an ingredient is created that helps sustain their marriage. This ingredient, created by God, is a powerful "one-flesh" connection between the marriage partners. When God created Adam and Eve, He first created Adam from the dust of the ground, then Eve, using tissue from Adam's body. In Genesis 2:23 Adam declared that Eve was "bone of my bones…" In the next verse the author of Genesis declares that all subsequent marriages will share the same *one-flesh* bond as that of the first couple. Genesis 2:24 says: *Therefore a man shall leave his father and mother and be joined to his wife, and they shall become one flesh.*

Relationships between best friends may be described as loving, but the union between a husband and wife is much deeper. The powerful connection between a married couple sets them apart in a one-flesh bond that makes the relationship exclusive and distinct. We call this powerful connection a nuclear bond.

This same nuclear bond exists between parents and their children. When a child is born, a powerful lifetime biological bond is formed between child and parent. Parents may establish close loving relationships with other children, but those relationships do not compare with the connection parents have with their own children.[1]

The bond between parents and children and the bond between married couples are considered to be identical. The Bible makes no distinction between the two. The one-flesh bond between a couple is considered by the Bible to be the same as the one-flesh bond between parents and their children.

Even though two non-related adults come together in marriage, it is fascinating that the Bible declares them bonded with a nuclear bond just like the bond between parents and their children.

We find this to be true in our own marriages. From the time of our marriage we no longer view ourselves independently from each other. We see our partners not separately but as extensions of ourselves.

The power of this bond becomes clearly evident when the bond is broken. Ending a friendship probably won't cause someone to seek therapy, but ending a marriage can and often does. The disruption of marital bonds can have disastrous emotional and psychological consequences. You can work closely with a co-worker for decades and feel very sad if he or she leaves the company. But if your marriage partner deserts you, even after only a few months of marriage, you may feel the loss for the rest of your life. Why? Because the deep, powerful marital bond that so connected you and your partner was torn apart, leaving you in deep trauma and terrible suffering.

The priority of the nuclear bond

We call the connections between married adults and between parents and their children nuclear bonds because they are central in people's lives and critical to their future well-being.

Is the nuclear bond a physical, biological bond? Yes, it is! But it is more than that. Is it an emotional bond as well? Is the bond a psychological and spiritual connection? Absolutely! And is the nuclear bond a cultural and social connection, too? Again, yes, and much, much more. The nuclear bond is at the very core of an individual's life. This family bond is *the* foundation for developing emotionally healthy, happy, well-adjusted individuals.

Like nuclear energy, the power of nuclear bonds holds the potential for indescribable good and indescribable horror for family members. If the bonds are cared for, they can be of tremendous benefit to people throughout their lives. If ignored and disrespected, the damaged bonded relationships can cause individuals a lifetime of emotional suffering.

A chaplain from a state prison told me his office offers greeting cards free of charge to prisoners to send to their loved ones at various holidays. The chaplaincy pays for all the cards and postage. Recently in a prison with 5,000 inmates the chaplain distributed literally thousands of Mother's Day cards. The next month he distributed cards to the prisoners for Father's Day. The chaplain then asked me to guess how many prisoners requested cards to send to their fathers.

After thinking about it, I guessed maybe 10 percent of the prisoners, or about 500, took cards.

Shaking his head, the chaplain held up both hands. The number of prisoners who asked for Father's Day cards was less than ten—fewer than 10 out of 5,000 inmates!

I was amazed. I wondered aloud to the chaplain how many of the prisoners would be incarcerated today if their fathers had been attentive and caring.

The chaplain told me that if fathers did their job, the prison would have to close down for lack of business.

Time and again it has been proven that emotional health and stability are centered in the nuclear bond. Certainly people can develop normally in the care of persons other than their own parents, but overwhelmingly we see that it is the relationships among bonded family members that largely determine stability or instability in individuals. If your nuclear bonded relationships are maintained and cared for, you can build in yourself and in your children lasting stability and emotional health.

Powerful loyalties

One of the most powerful aspects of the nuclear bond is the loyalty it creates among family members. Nuclear bonds establish your place in life and give you your identity. It's because of the nuclear bond that a child says, "This is not just a dad, this is *my* dad. This is not just a mother, this is *my* mother. This is *my* brother, *my* sister."

Nuclear bonds also identify who is *not* a family member. Who else has open access to your home, your food, your dinner table, your family room? Can just anyone walk in, eat, leave a plate and cup on the counter top, and then lie down on the couch and watch television? Can just anyone use your electricity, your water, or drive your car? Few people outside your nuclear bonds have those privileges. Why? Because they aren't part of your biological connections, your nuclear bonds.

It's because of nuclear bonds that you love and support your spouse. It is because of nuclear bonds that you serve your children: cling to them, support them, favor them, discipline them, cuddle them, and, at times, let them get by with murder. It is because of nuclear bonds that you recognize your immediate family as more than just people close to you—you recognize them as *part of yourself—you*! Doesn't the following sound familiar?

- If some kid cries too much, the parent is irresponsible and ought to quiet the kid down. If *your* child cries too much, the child has a good reason and everyone should feel sympathetic.

- If someone is fired, he or she probably deserved it. If *your* spouse is fired, the employer made a foolish mistake and will live to regret the error.

- If another child is a rising star, she is probably conceited and shouldn't be overly praised. If *your* child is the star of the class, everyone should notice and congratulate your child.

- If an umpire calls a kid out at home plate, the kid is out. If an umpire calls *your* kid out, he is incompetent and should volunteer his time somewhere else.

- If an officer gives a guy a speeding ticket, the driver deserves everything that's coming to him. If an officer gives *your* spouse a speeding ticket, the officer is just trying to fill his quota of tickets for the week.

Everyone *thinks* his or her child will become the next superstar, the next famous author, the next renowned scientist, the next great church leader—or the President of the United States. But yours *will!*

～

Making Your Blending Family Work

Nuclear bonds are the absolute seat of emotional health through which children and parents can develop stable, happy lives.

2

WHY MERGING TWO FAMILIES SO OFTEN FAILS
The Problem with Joining Nuclear Bonds

W hy are some family members rejected in a remarriage? Why can't everyone just get along? Recognizing and understanding the bonds in your own blending family is the *first* step in building a peaceful blending family.

Demand for independence by nuclear bonds

Nuclear bonds—biological connections—are fiercely loyal to their own family members and demand independence from other bonds. Bonds want to be alone and exclusive. They don't like joining in with other bonded relationships. Look up and down any street and you will see that families live in separate houses and apartments, not in communal homes. Why? Because nuclear bonds are private and strive to live with just those of their own biology.

Bonds are not designed to merge or overlap; they're designed to be independent and co-exist with each other. You see it when couples get married. Now that they have formed their bond, they want to live together on their own and be totally independent.

Imagine the problems created for a couple if one of the spouses continues to be tied to a parent. This is what is happening to Craig and Suze following their marriage. It is a first marriage for both; yet Craig, the new husband, isn't ready to let go of his parents.

Craig is allowing his mother to intrude into his marriage, which is causing severe difficulties. For example, when Craig and Suze were making plans for a vacation, Suze was horrified to learn that Craig's parents had already invited themselves along and Craig had accepted without Suze's agreement.

Suze is adamant that Craig stand up to his mother and not allow her so much influence in their lives.

Are we surprised to learn that Suze is having difficulty with her new mother-in-law? No. The nuclear bond of Craig and Suze is demanding separation and independence. They need to operate under their own authority. They need independence because the nuclear bond established at the time of their marriage immediately resists overlapping with other bonds.

On a smaller scale, don't you experience a desire for independence when you stay with friends or relatives for an extended period? Even when you're just visiting for a few hours or a few days, the forces of the bonds can cause tensions. Visiting may be fun, but outstaying your welcome can become difficult for everyone.

If merged bonds don't function very well with visiting relatives, if they don't work well between Craig and Suze and Craig's parents, how then are you going to manage them in your blending family?

Understanding why stepfamilies have difficulties

In first marriages couples intentionally separate from all outside nuclear bonds. That brings peace.

In blending marriages there is intentional *overlapping* of bonds. That brings automatic difficulty and hardship.

One very positive characteristic about nuclear bonds is that they generate loyalty among family members. But this loyalty can spell doom for blending families as the loyalty is toward bonded family members and not toward persons who try to join the family.

Nuclear bonds work extremely well for first marriages because all the members share the same biological bond.

In contrast, blending families may have three, four, eight, or more multiple bonds (biological bonds) overlapping each other, each bond favoring its own members and resisting non-family members.

The nuclear bonds are identified in the families below.

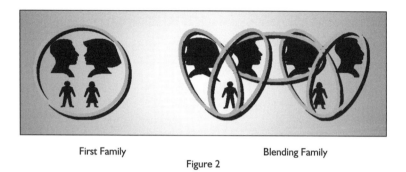

First Family   Blending Family

Figure 2

The couple in the first marriage share one bond and enjoy their independence. In the blending family, however, there are five overlapping bonds: the couple, each parent and child, and the children's bonds with their other parents, all of the bonds naturally opposing one another.

In a first marriage there is a common bond and shared loyalty among all of the family members. In the blending family, loyalties also exist, but *only to persons in their own bonds*—favoring their own bonds and rejecting family members outside the bonds.

It's when other people start telling you they are now part of your family and start living in your home that causes nuclear bonds to revolt. By design, the force of loyalty and the natural rejection of outsiders create divisions among blending members. It is the nuclear bond that is at the very heart of why blending families have such problems.

Why nuclear bonds work in some relationships and not in others

Even though the design of nuclear bonds is to favor their own members and hold at arm's length non-nuclear members, people in the family respond to nuclear bonds differently. Bonded members don't all love one another, and non-bonded members don't all hate one another.

Married couples divorce, and some parents and children will never speak to each other again. Stepparents and stepkids may have a truly loving relationship.

The question is why. Why are some stepfamilies loving and happy and others constantly at each other's throats?

The answer is that nuclear bonds are either awakened into loyalty toward their own members and rejecting outsiders or quieted allowing acceptance and peaceful co-existence.

If the bonds are awakened, non-biological family members will never connect and will always be involved in some level of nuclear war. If quieted, non-biological family members can connect and form a loving blending family.

The road to peace for every blending family

If nuclear bonds are awakened, they will immediately go to work rejecting and expelling non-biological family members, causing havoc in your blending family. The bonds do not consider who gets hurt or devastated or emotionally scarred for life. They will not cease their work until everyone is segregated according to biological lines. The most critical objective of every blending family is to keep nuclear bonds quiet.

Successful blending families with quieted bonds minimize biological lines and treat everyone in the family like a biological member. Blending families with awakened bonds experience serious difficulties as family members become acutely aware of, and opposed to, non-biological lines. The extent to which the bonds are kept quiet largely determines the peace and happiness level of everyone in your family.

∽

Making Your Blending Family Work

Awakened nuclear bonds unify biological members against outsiders.

Learning to quiet them is key to achieving a peaceful and successful blending family.

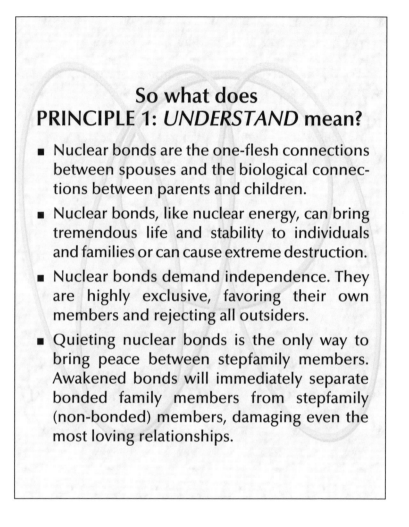

So what does
PRINCIPLE 1: *UNDERSTAND* mean?

- Nuclear bonds are the one-flesh connections between spouses and the biological connections between parents and children.

- Nuclear bonds, like nuclear energy, can bring tremendous life and stability to individuals and families or can cause extreme destruction.

- Nuclear bonds demand independence. They are highly exclusive, favoring their own members and rejecting all outsiders.

- Quieting nuclear bonds is the only way to bring peace between stepfamily members. Awakened bonds will immediately separate bonded family members from stepfamily (non-bonded) members, damaging even the most loving relationships.

Principle 2

IDENTIFY

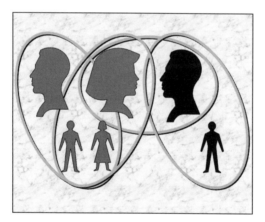

3

IDENTIFYING THE CRITICAL RELATIONSHIPS IN YOUR NEW FAMILY
Identifying All Bonds and Connections

The second principle in creating stepfamily health is to *identify* all nuclear bonds. Unlike first marriages wherein every member shares the same bond, in blending families bonds need to be clearly recognized. This is life in a blending family. What is taken for granted in first marriages must in blending families become the subject of careful and intense consideration. So, once you understand what nuclear bonds are, your next step is to identify them.

Identifying nuclear bonds and step-connections

If you asked first-marriage family members to name the people in their family, they would all list the same people: mother, father, sons, daughters, brothers and sisters. But if you asked people in a blending family to identify their family members, they would have a much harder time. Each blending family member would probably have a totally different take on who constitutes the family.

Things can get a bit complicated. Kids would ask, "Which family, my mom's or my dad's?" And family members might forget (or wish to forget) some of their bonds or step-connections: stepkids, stepmother, stepfather, or stepbrothers and -sisters. But every single one of these bonds and step-connections is critical to blending family health.

Identifying bonds means to recognize all the bonds directly associated with all the members of your family.

Nuclear bonds are identified because they are the most powerful relationships in the family, essential to the emotional health and stability of each member.

How many bonds do you see?

For starters, look at the blending family in Figure 3, below. This family consists of a woman with her two kids, her husband and his daughter, and the former spouses, currently single. To identify nuclear bonds, we've circled all the biological connections. We therefore see three bonds within the blending family and two outside, which are the other parents of the children. Both the wife and husband in this blending family have a total of five bonds among themselves and their children.

Figure 3

Let's talk step-connections. We must identify step-connections because they, too, hold keys to family happiness. Step-connections are the various non-biological relationships among children and adults and tend to destabilize quickly. Yet, stepfamily success is largely determined by the quality of the step-connections. We will discuss step-connections in future chapters. For now let's just identify them.

How many step-connections are there in this blending family? The married parents are stepparents to each other's children and there's one connection just between the kids (step-siblings), totaling three connections.

Add together the five bonds (shown) and three step-connections (not shown) and you will find a total of eight significant relationships seriously impacting the family. And this is just a simple, straight-forward, blending family!

Get out your pencil

How many nuclear bonds and step-connections are there among your family members? Sketch out your blending family as we did in our example. When you count bonds, remember that once divorced, the bond between a couple is broken, so you won't circle yourself and your former spouse. Be sure to include marriage partners in a biological bond. Partners living together are also considered to have a bonded relationship as they will impact your children and you. If a parent is deceased or has permanently abandoned the family, include that parent in your drawing. Children continue to feel a connection with and loyalty to an absent or deceased parent.

We are not including grandparents or relatives in the diagram even though they share your bloodline.

Parents and their children all share in one bond, regardless of the number of children. If a mother has three children from three different fathers, the mother and children are of the same biology, thus sharing one bond. The three kids have separate bonds with their own fathers. If a child has been adopted, include the child in a bond with the adoptive parents as if it were a biological bond. However, the biological parents of that child must also be acknowledged in separate bonds.

Drawing a diagram of your different family members may be painful for you, as you are forced to acknowledge or recall certain relationships. Try to separate yourself from your emotions when it comes to this exercise. Whether you approve or disapprove of certain individuals is not the issue. Whether your child sees the other parent or not is not the issue. What matters is whether these individuals are connected to your family through biological bonds. Absent parents or children will continue to have some impact on your family.

Identifying your step-connections

After diagraming your family, figure out how many step-connections there are. Include not only the step-connections of you and your partner but also the step-connections of your children. Is your children's other parent remarried? Is the other parent living with someone or in a long-term relationship? Does that new partner have any children? Include all of these as step-connections.

Step-connections are as critical to a stepfamily's emotional health and stability as the family's biological bonds. Healthy step-connections are absolutely essential to the overall well-being of any blending family. If the step-connections are positive, the blending family is probably doing well. If the step-connections are negative or difficult, the family as a whole is probably suffering.

In contrast to nuclear bonds which favor their members, step-connections tend to oppose and to drive members away from one another. For example, introduce a new parent to your kids and you'll probably face some opposition. The point is that these powerful connections need to be identified and given serious attention.

How many step-connections are there in your family? Add that number to the number of nuclear bonds. That total number may be quite an eye-opener. If your blending family is to find the happiness you desire, each nuclear bond and step-connection will require individual attention.

Why go to all the trouble of identifying bonds and step-connections?

Why is it important to recognize nuclear bonds and step-connections? Because identification is extremely important in quieting the powerful nuclear bonds and easing step-connections. Every one of these relationships has the potential to bring your family either happiness and emotional health or incredible misery. The bonds are poised at any moment to spill out their toxins and destroy the emotional stability of you and your children. By their very design they oppose overlapping and want to split apart from one another. They are too powerful to leave to themselves. They need to be identified, separated out, satisfied, and quieted.

What you will want to do is transform them from possible centers of harm into centers of health and peace.

This is the second universe, doing whatever it takes to make the bonds and step-relationships of your blending family as peaceful as possible. They *can* be calmed and quieted. This is the second principle in the art of loving your stepfamily.

Just for fun: Figure out the bonds and connections

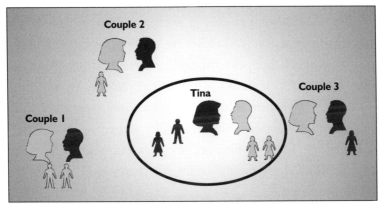

Figure 4

Can you figure out the number of bonds in Tina's blending family? Here's the setting. Tina is in her third marriage. Tina had a daughter in her first marriage. Her ex-husband remarried and he and his wife (Couple 1) have two sons. Then Tina married another fellow and had a son with him. Following her second divorce her ex-husband remarried a woman with a daughter (Couple 2). Now in her third marriage, Tina's new blending family consists of four kids—her daughter and son who live with her and her new husband, and two stepdaughters who live primarily with their mother.

It's a second marriage for Tina's husband. His former wife is currently living with her boyfriend and the boyfriend's daughter (Couple 3). Tina's husband's daughters live with their mother and see their father and Tina a couple of weekends a month.

Can you figure out the nuclear bonds and step-connections in this complicated family? How many are there? Try to identify them all before reading the solution below.

We count a total of eleven nuclear bonded relationships: seven biological bonds between the children and their parents and four bonds between the three married couples and the couple living together. We also count seven step-connections between stepparents and stepchildren and three stepchild connections[1] among these families, totaling ten step-connections. The total number of bonds and step-connections connected to Tina's family comes to twenty-one!

Tina and her husband need immediate and critical help in understanding how to properly manage themselves and their family members in this potentially explosive environment with so many nuclear bonds and step-connections.

All of these bonded relationships and step-connections, even the couple living together, are extremely important to identify. *Every one of these bonds and connections is critical to the life and well-being of Tina's blending family.* If any one of these relationships is troubled, there can be serious negative consequences for Tina, her children, and her spouse and children.

Creating well-functioning blending families requires preparation, understanding, and the ability to work with powerful forces—in other words, there is need for a high level of negotiation, management, and conflict-resolution skills. It is critical that all of these bonds and connections be quieted down and brought under control. Now you know why blending families can't operate by the rules of a first marriage.

By the way, in our blending family Jenetha and I have thirteen nuclear bonds, seven step-connections, and four step-child connections totaling twenty-four bonds and step-connections. When we say that blending families can't operate by the rules of a first marriage, we're not kidding.

Identifying the bonds and step-connections is the second principle in building a successful stepfamily. Now that you've separated your blending family into its biological ties and step-connections, you can focus on specific relationships and learn how to make them work.

∾

Making Your Blending Family Work

Your family is defined today by the people who are part of your blending and extended family. Identification of every bond and step-connection is critical to making your blending family work.

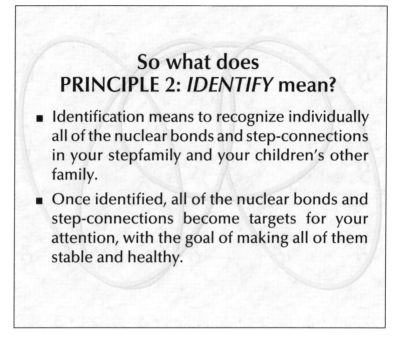

So what does PRINCIPLE 2: *IDENTIFY* mean?

- Identification means to recognize individually all of the nuclear bonds and step-connections in your stepfamily and your children's other family.

- Once identified, all of the nuclear bonds and step-connections become targets for your attention, with the goal of making all of them stable and healthy.

Principle 3

ACCEPT

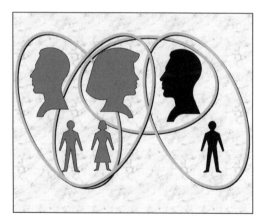

4

ACCEPTING YOUR CHILDREN'S OTHER PARENT INTO THEIR LIVES

Accepting All Outside Bonds and Connections

Acceptance is the third principle in the art of making your blending family work.

Once you have identified your family relationships, which are all your bonds and step-connections, your next goal is to *accept* these relationships, not oppose them. Easier said than done (yes, we know!).

Accepting bonds and step-connections means that you allow the other parents and stepparents the full rights and privileges due them. Acceptance means that you honor these relationships as fact and you leave them alone, without any negative interference from you or your children.

Acceptance means allowing other adults to live their own lives in the way they see fit. This includes parents living together, parents who act irresponsibly in their relationships, and/or parents who have minimal ability to manage their work, finances, or themselves.

Acceptance does not mean approval! Because you accept the rights of parents to manage their own children doesn't mean you approve of them or their method of child-raising. But the *position* of biological parent and stepparent is to be highly respected and honored by you and your children, whether earned or not. Every parent and every stepparent is to be considered important and vital to the emotional well-being of your children.

It is common for parents to criticize their former spouses and the spouse's partner. A mother says to her kids, "Who knows what worthless person your father is dating this time." Even if the individual dating the former spouse seems to be quite decent, some parents feel that he or she is disqualified from earning their respect. But such words and attitudes are harmful to your kids.

If there is no threat of abuse or physical harm to your children, and because you have no way of controlling your former spouse's dating choices, *acceptance* is the only productive way of handling these relationships. For all of your bonds and connections to remain quiet, and for the emotional health of your kids, you must accept all outside relationships, whether you approve of them or not.

Failure to respect a nuclear bond

Success in your blending family is as dependent on your accepting the non-family members outside your blending family as it is on accepting the members of your own family. Whether or not you like the people in your children's other family, *every* bond and *every* step-connection is a key element in promoting your children's well-being, as well as your own stepfamily happiness.

Dave went through a messy divorce with his now ex-wife, who abandoned the children, moved out of the state, and over the next few years saw her three young children less than once a month.

When Dave then married Jodi, he considered her the perfect woman to become his children's new mother. She was stable, loving, and cared a great deal for the children—everything his ex-wife wasn't.

A year after their marriage, the children's mother called to say she wanted the children to come live with her. Dave told her she had lost that privilege and that the children now had a real mother.

A long, protracted court battle ensued. During the litigation, the mother influenced the children to say some untrue things about Jodi and their father to the court mediator.

The allegations caused the court to decide in favor of the mother. Today, Dave and Jodi are consumed with bitterness toward the court and the mother and feel betrayed by the children.

Dave is wondering what kind of relationship to have with his kids, whether he should even call them during the week. For now, Jodi won't even talk to them. Both Dave and Jodi feel that the children owe them a huge explanation of why they spoke against them in court. As of now, there is little conversation between the father and his kids and a lot of heartache.

What went wrong and what can be done now?

Dave and Jodi were shocked to experience the re-awakening of the nuclear bond between the mother and her children. Instead of *adding* Jodi as a mother figure, Dave had tried to *replace* the biological mother. Dave and Jodi had refused to identify or accept the nuclear bond between the kids and their mother and had worked hard to erase the memory of it.

But nuclear bonds cannot be erased.

Bonds demand recognition, and their loyalties will force acceptance, as Dave and Jodi found out.

If Dave and his wife had understood the critical importance of the nuclear bond, and had identified and accepted the nuclear bond between the children and their mother, they would have understood the children's need for their mother. Dave and his wife would have tried to find some way for the mother to become more involved in the children's lives. They would have understood that his children were suffering mentally and emotionally from not being with their mother.

For the sake of the children's emotional health, when the mother did express interest in seeing her children more, Dave and Jodi should have done what they could to insure that the mother had easy access to her children.

It was wise of Dave to be cautious about the sudden return of the children's mother, to be protective of his kids, and to watch over their well-being. But he needed to encourage the mom's attachment.

The mother's involvement will surely cause Dave and Jodi more problems and frustration. But the benefits to the children of enjoying the attention of both parents will far outweigh any difficulties. Having children fully engaged with both parents, even if one parent continues to be difficult, is still healthier for them than no other parent at all.

Dave and Jodi should not have focused on their own needs or wants or desires, but only on what would fully satisfy the nuclear bonds and the emotional health of his children.

So where do Dave and Jodi go from here? They will need to accept the reality of the children's mother and the need of the children to be with both parents. Dave and Jodi must understand, identify, and accept the mother's nuclear bond with her kids.

Forget the hurtful words of the kids

Should Dave's kids be required to own up to and apologize for what they said against Dave and Jodi to the court mediator?

Absolutely not! They're kids! They did what they did for their mother. It's unjust and emotionally harmful for Dave or Jodi to even think of punishing the children.

Come on! The kids were caught between warring parents. Legal battles between parents put the children in a no-win situation. Whatever they say in favor of one parent is taken as treason by the other. How damaging to the kids!

To move forward, Dave and Jodi need to develop, above everything else, a total case of amnesia—forgetting about the negative things the mother and children said against them in court. They must accept the mother and pursue a course of reconciliation, humility, and kindness toward their emotionally battered children.

Amnesia is sometimes a critical element of success!

To be successful in baseball, every pitcher must learn to play with amnesia. If he throws the wrong pitch and the batter hits one out of the park, the pitcher must put the home run out of his mind. He has to step off the mound, re-chalk his hands, take his glove off and put it back on, and tell himself it's a new day, a new game, and a new batter. He has to will himself to forget about the home run and face the next batter as if it were the first one of the game. If he doesn't, he'll begin throwing under pressure, get out of rhythm, and start to make huge mistakes.

If a major league pitcher can't pitch with amnesia, he won't continue in the majors.

So it is with blending parents—if they can't develop amnesia, they will bring their family to ruin.

There are so many bonds and step-connections in every blending family that just the sheer number of people involved will result in someone saying the wrong thing at the wrong time. It's inevitable! And with all the parents and stepparents trying to influence the kids to their way of thinking, it is understandable that the kids will say and do things against one adult to please another.

If you catalog and remember every injustice done to you by a child, or stepchild, or adult, your family absolutely will not thrive. Blending families are filled with injustice! Having a memory like an elephant will only lead to disaster.

You may have been seriously hurt by something someone has said and your injured feelings may be totally justified. Nevertheless, if you don't develop amnesia and don't accept all the bonds and step-connections, you'll hurt yourself and damage your children emotionally.

Even if you thoroughly disapprove, dislike, and are disgusted with the nuclear bonded adults connected to your family, you must accept them and, like the pitcher, learn to live with amnesia.

What if there is immorality?
What if the other parent is irresponsible?

Let's say your ex-spouse has found a live-in partner. What are you to do? Can you influence the dating choices of your ex-spouse? Can you force your irresponsible former partner to be responsible? Can you alter your former spouse's character, lifestyle, or habits? No. You can't do anything to change the life-style of your ex.

You can choose to criticize, to complain, and to bemoan the situation, telling your children how terrible their other parent is, condemning the parent to family and friends.

Or, you can accept the realities of a situation out of your control, thereby calming your own emotions and those of your children, and show them how to react to such difficulties by your example.

Peter writes in the Bible: "*...be tenderhearted, be courteous; not returning evil for evil or reviling for reviling, but on the contrary blessing, knowing that you were called to this, that you may inherit a blessing. For "He who would love life and see good days, let him refrain his tongue from evil, and his lips from speaking deceit. Let him turn away from evil and do good; let him seek peace and pursue it.*"[1]

Peter is saying, in effect, that regardless of whatever is done against you, you can control your response.

Then what should be your response? The Bible is telling you that your response is to accept the relationship as part of your children's family and to be kind, considerate, and helpful—and to instruct your children to act in the same way.

When Nathan and his wife divorced, custody of their young daughter was granted to the mother. Nathan had only limited visitation rights.

The mother deliberately worked to turn the daughter's heart against her father by convincing her that Nathan was the cause of all their unhappiness and problems. To Nathan's deep heartache, following her mother's example, his daughter rejected him.

When the daughter turned sixteen, she rebelled, moved out of her mother's home, and began living with friends. Nathan thought this might be an opportunity to try to re-connect with his daughter. He called his daughter and invited her out to dinner. He told his daughter that he just wanted to spend time with her.

To Nathan's surprise, his daughter agreed to have dinner with him.

Their first meeting went extremely well. Nathan listened to his daughter and didn't challenge her in any way. They agreed that every Wednesday evening he would take her out to dinner.

Nathan made sure that he picked her up about the same time and took her to the same restaurant they both enjoyed. He wanted his daughter to experience a few hours of stability, tradition, and safety—something that was severely lacking in her life.

His plan worked perfectly. They became well-known regulars at the restaurant and even got to be friends with the waiters. Nathan made sure that their time together was a safe haven for his daughter. He never spoke negatively toward his daughter's mother. In fact, he always supported his ex-wife and spoke kindly about her if her name came up in conversation.

And this went on for about a year.

Is it any wonder that today Nathan and his daughter are about as close as any daughter and father could be? Is it any wonder that this young woman eventually became a wonderful, responsible person who now also has a good relationship with her mother?

Nathan accepted the nuclear bonds. He developed amnesia regarding his ex-wife and his daughter's past behavior and words. He concentrated only on restoring his relationship with his daughter and nourishing her emotional health. Nathan explained that God his Father had forgiven him a lifetime of trespasses and errors so he could certainly forgive his ex-wife and daughter of their trespasses against him.

―――――――――――――― ∾ ――――――――――――――

Making Your Blending Family Work

Accept all bonds and step-connections. "God has called us to peace."

I Corinthians 7:15

5

ACCEPTING YOUR SPOUSE'S CHILDREN INTO YOUR LIFE
Accepting All Inside Connections

Accepting all bonds and step-connections means not only accepting all bonds and connections *outside* your blending family but *inside* the family, too. This means that you accept *all* of your blending family members—which can be surprisingly difficult.

Rejection among stepfamily members is so common that it seems to be standard practice in stepfamilies. Stepparents reject their stepchildren and stepchildren reject their stepparents. Parents even reject their own children in favor of a new spouse and a new family. And children may even reject a parent or stepparent.

We're not saying that everyone has to love everyone in a blending family. That may be unrealistic. But all family members should at least have a basic civil respect for one another.

Much unhappiness in blending families is caused by the alienation or rejection of certain family members. What you must do is recognize and accept all bonds and step-connections within your blending family. We're suggesting that *you* set the example. Somebody needs to start the process of health in the family.

Accepting your own kids

Both teenagers were seventeen when they married. They quickly had two children, a daughter and a son, but then divorced soon after. As young single parents neither the mother nor the father could adequately care for the kids, so they sent them to live with the mother's parents. Once freed of the daily responsibilities of child care, the father and mother lived as carefree single adults. Eventually both found new partners, remarried, and established new families.

Today, neither the father nor the mother has much to do with their first daughter and son, and the children have been pretty much abandoned to the care of the grandparents. When the children do see their parents, it is at the parents' convenience.

When the father was asked why he doesn't try to see his children, the father replied, "It hurts me too much."

The son now refuses to see or speak with his mother or father, but the daughter continues to try to keep in touch, calling her parents separately and trying to see them every few months. When the daughter does manage to connect with her mother or father, both parents talk about themselves and appear uninterested in what is going on in their daughter's life. The mother talks constantly about the children she has with her current husband. The dad is only interested in himself.

The nuclear bonds between the parents and the children have been incredibly injured. What is supposed to be a center of emotional health and stability for the children has become a source of damage. The very foundation of the children's life has been rejected and shattered. Is it any wonder the 16-year-old daughter dresses and acts like a worldly 25-year-old woman? Is it surprising that her 15-year-old brother is struggling with drug abuse and is in and out of rehab for troubled teens?

Fortunately, the children do have their grandparents, adults who care for them and try to provide some stability in their lives. Yet, the obvious rejection of the parents continues to deflate the children emotionally.

Because of the nuclear bond's capability to destroy or to restore emotional health, God commands every parent and every child to reconcile. Malachi 4:6 says: *And he will turn the hearts of the fathers to the children, and the hearts of the children to their fathers, lest I come and strike the earth with a curse.* In effect, Malachi is saying that regardless of the age of the parent or child, full reconciliation and restoration should take place (if there is no danger to the child or parent).

The mother and father and their marriage partners are required by God to heal the breach and immediately invest time and energy in their first daughter and son. The mother and father have the responsibility to restore stability in the lives of their two struggling children.

Accepting your stepchildren

When Calvin and Kathleen married, Calvin moved into Kathleen's home. Just a few days after their honeymoon, Kathleen's 14-year-old daughter, who was living with her father, asked if she could come and live with her mother. Kathleen readily agreed.

The decision caught Calvin totally off guard. He didn't want the girl intruding into his marriage. He never imagined that within a few days of their marriage he would be a full-time stepparent to Kathleen's daughter.

Calvin's solution was to try to make things as unpleasant as possible so that the daughter would return to her father's house. But she didn't leave. Instead, she became extremely hostile to Calvin and quickly turned against him.

Calvin saw that the daughter wasn't about to go back to her father, so he then tried to turn Kathleen against her daughter. To Calvin's amazement, Kathleen reacted like the daughter. Instead of siding with Calvin the mother sided with her daughter, becoming hostile against him. The marriage ended two weeks later.

Fatal errors

Calvin's first fatal error was never considering that the daughter would be a factor in his marriage to Kathleen. It never occurred to him that the girl might move in with them—or that she might stay for years! Calvin needed to have thought through the various scenarios regarding his wife's child before he and Kathleen ever married.

Calvin's other fatal error was disrespecting the bond between the mom and her daughter. Calvin's arrogance awakened the powerful nuclear bond between mother and daughter and cost him his marriage.

Accepting a very troubled stepchild

What if the *child* refuses to accept the marital bond between parent and stepparent?

When I met Cheryl and Brian, Cheryl's eldest daughter was sixteen years old. What had begun as a reasonable relationship years ago had now deteriorated to the point where the daughter had completely rejected Brian. Both Brian and Cheryl were at a loss as to how to manage their blending family when the daughter would have nothing to do with her stepdad.

Somehow over several years the nuclear bond with the daughter was awakened and continues to remain awake. And the awakened bond is creating havoc against the non-nuclear member of the family, the stepfather.

Whatever caused the awakening of the bond must be investigated. Is another family member influencing the girl against Brian for some reason? Is Cheryl, Brian's own wife, without realizing it, doing something to turn her daughter against him? Is the problem Brian's fault? Has he said or done anything to cause the stepdaughter to withdraw from him? Or, does the daughter just have such a strong sense of loyalty to her parents that it keeps her nuclear bond awake? All of these things need to be explored, because something is causing the nuclear bond to remain active.

To save his marriage Brian must—absolutely must—walk through this grim experience with amnesia, forgetting the harsh actions and words spoken against him by the daughter. He needs to develop an optimistic outlook for the daughter and anticipate a good relationship in the future. In doing so, he will be able to enjoy the daughter when the bond quiets down.

Brian may just have to wait this one out until the daughter matures.

For now, Brian can focus on the nuclear bond between Cheryl, the mother, and her daughter. He can see to it that they have the opportunity and time to do enjoyable things together. He can also try to encourage the daughter's relationship with her father. What Brian must *not* do is give up on his stepdaughter, try to move her out of the house, or try to cause any separation between her and her mother. He must accept their bond and ride out the storm.

Parent authority

In the first years of marriage, stepparents need to do what they can to support parent-child relationships. This will go far in keeping nuclear bonds quiet. Stepparents can negotiate and make changes but must do so through the biological parent, gradually introducing new traditions and lifestyles. Parents exercising their own authority and controls will not arouse the nuclear bond.

Whatever the case, stepparents absolutely must not interfere with the nuclear bond. That includes trying to threaten it, control it, or damage it. Accepting nuclear bonds is the only way to keep them manageable.

Accepting your adult stepchildren

Margaret and David married in December, close to the Christmas holidays. She moved in with her husband, who was quite well off and had a beautiful home with a detached guesthouse. His two grown sons and one adult daughter were all married and living out of state. All planned to fly in to be with their father and Margaret during Christmas. Since Margaret had an artistic flair, she decided to decorate David's house to the max for the occasion.

When the grown children and their families arrived, the reactions of delight Margaret had expected were completely absent. In fact, her decorating efforts were met with silence and obvious disapproval. David's kids had expected to see the familiar holiday decorations they had always enjoyed during their childhood. What they saw instead was a holiday showpiece better suited to a New York department store.

Margaret was disappointed in the children's reactions but didn't let it affect her.

Margaret let David and his children know that this was her house now and she would decorate it the way she pleased.

Margaret is now gone. The couple divorced shortly after the holidays.

Acquisition vs. merger

Margaret entered the family like a new boss who wasn't about to tiptoe around her employees. She had goals and plans and made them happen.

But a blending family isn't like a business *acquisition* where one company has control and dictates orders to another. Blending a family is like a business *merger* where everyone has to go through the painstaking time and energy to communicate with one another, build relationships, and work together as changes are made.

In her bid for acquisition Margaret in effect announced to David's kids that she had arrived, was in charge, and they had better get used to the idea.

Instead of accepting the nuclear bonds she challenged them. There was only one relationship that mattered and that was the relationship between her and David. She had little comprehension of the powerful nuclear connections between the father and his children. Because the children were grown, Margaret never considered the permanent influence of the biological bonds between parent and children.

If she had identified and accepted the bonds between the father and his children, and had understood the power of those connections, she would not have entered the family like a boss in acquisition. Instead she would have called the adult children, discussed the upcoming holiday with them, and asked if there was anything about Christmas that they particularly enjoyed or anything she could do to make Christmas special.

Relationships are everything in blending families. *Acceptance* and *service* are the attitudes that quiet nuclear bonds and allow families to prosper. Force, control, and trying to get one's way only awaken nuclear bonds and damage relationships.

In awakening the nuclear bonds against her, Margaret doomed her marriage.

~

Making Your Blending Family Work

Accepting nuclear bonds and stepconnections inside your family means to see to it that all family members are respected.

6

THE TRUE ROLE OF THE STEPPARENT

Accepting the Stepparent as a Stepparent

Practically all stepparents enter into their blending families with the highest expectations and confidence that they will love their stepchildren. They rush in thinking they will be the loving parent the children never had—only to find that things don't turn out the way they had imagined.

Step-connection relationships in blending families tend to travel up and down like a roller coaster, fluctuating between positive and negative many times over. When the relationships are good, the family functions smoothly and happily. But when the relationships turn bad, and stay sour, they have a terrible effect on the climate and mood of the entire family.

To love me is to love my children

One man told his wife that if she loved him, she would also love his 8-year-old daughter. The wife agreed with this, fully expecting that she would love the daughter as her own.

But problems immediately arose when the daughter became bossy and hard to control. When the girl didn't obey the stepmother's corrections, the stepmom turned to the father for help. But the father told her the daughter was just being a child and to overlook the bad behavior, as any biological parent, on occasion, might do.

The problem was that the stepmother wasn't conditioned to behave like a biological parent. As time progressed, the stepmother wanted less and less to do with her stepdaughter. And the guilt the stepmother experienced because of her negative feelings toward the girl was overwhelming.

She knew that if she told her husband how she felt, he would be shocked and disappointed. She also knew it might seriously compromise his feelings toward her. So the stepmother was stuck in her own private war, battling terribly negative feelings toward the child, her own feelings of guilt and failure, and the fear of the withdrawal of her husband.

Parents cannot require a stepparent to duplicate a parent's biological love. For the parent to tell his new spouse, "To love me is to love my children," is to program the relationship for certain failure. The love of a stepparent cannot be expected or forced. And it should never be measured against the love of a biological relationship.

The true expectation for parents and stepparents is not "to love me is to love my children" but *"to love you is to help you love your own children."*

Unrealistic expectations

Expecting parental behavior from a stepparent will do more to undermine a marriage relationship than anything else in a blending family. Accepting step-connections inside the blending family means to accept the reality that the stepparent cannot be obligated to act like a bio-parent or to take on the responsibility for someone else's kids.

Many parents believe that their new partners will suddenly be transformed into loving parents to their new stepchildren. Men expect their wives to love their children—and the wives are sure they will! Women expect nothing less of themselves. And women dream of men who will become great dads to their children.

Stepparenting usually doesn't work the way we imagine it will. Things can quickly become quite complicated and often pretty dismal.

The solution is to begin slowly, with few expectations. Do not imagine that your new spouse will instantly connect with your own children the way a nuclear parent would. It is far better for stepparents to be allowed to ease slowly into the job of stepparenting—to start gradually and let relationships develop at their own pace.

In fact, parents will want to acknowledge their partner's *lack* of biological connections to their own children. Parents who are willing to do the parenting and not depend on the new partner will start the blending family off on the right foot.

Stepparents, on the other hand, should *require* the bio-parent to continue parenting, with little obligation on themselves. Stepparents are then free to build whatever relationship they want with the children. The hope is for full and unhindered parenting by the stepparent, one day to be recognized and accepted as a co-parent.

The model for great stepparenting: Grandparents!

In the new universe of blending families, stepparenting is more like, or should be more like, the relationship between grandparents and grandkids—all pleasure and little *required* work. The secret to successful stepparenting is the same as the secret to successful grand-parenting: sincere gratitude by parents for anything they do for the children.

Think about how grandparents are treated. Everything they do is appreciated by the parents. Are grandparents expected to clean the house when they arrive? Are they required to do the shopping, cooking, or laundry? Are they supposed to discipline the children? Parents know that they are the ones—not the grandparents—who are responsible for their own children.

If grandparents do help, it's because they want to and are allowed to. But grandparents also know that at any time they can stop and hand over all responsibilities to the parents. No requirements! And the parents are still grateful for whatever the grandparents have contributed to the family.

And look at the welcome grandparents receive when they arrive! When the grandparents walk in the door, the parent feels a sense of relief, happiness, and thankfulness. And this thankfulness is *communicated*, which makes the grandparents want to come more often and do more for the family.

Yet the entire spirit of grandparenting can suddenly change if the parent *obligates* the grandparent to work and stops appreciating the grandparent's help. Suddenly the grandparent's feelings toward helping out around the house will change. The feeling is one of being used. The fun fades, and the responsibilities become heavy and exhausting.

Parents need to allow stepparents to operate under the same sense of freedom that grandparents have. Stepparents need to know that they are not under any obligation, and that if they do anything for their stepchildren, they will be appreciated and praised for their efforts.

Parents and stepparents need to agree that at the most fundamental level of their blending family, it is the parent who is in charge and it is the parent who bears the responsibility for his or her own children.

In one blending family, the kitchen is always left a mess after the kids fly through it, so the stepmother turns to the dad for a solution. She wants him to instruct his kids to put all the dirty dishes in the dishwasher and wipe the counters clean before leaving the kitchen.

The father tells the stepmother that she is way too particular about the kitchen. He thinks a dish left here or there isn't that big a deal and doesn't see why his new wife can't just clean up without complaining and making things so difficult.

Questions: *Who is having fun and feels at ease with how things are going in this family? The dad. Who's becoming discouraged? The stepmother.*

Now, who should have the least amount of built-in responsibility? The stepmom. And who should either clean the kitchen regularly or see to it that the kids clean up their mess? The dad.

But everything is turned around. After marriage this dad considers himself free to spend extra time at work instead of picking up the kids like he used to. On weekends he thinks he is now free to play golf. But the stepmother is feeling tired and unappreciated. These are not her children—she doesn't have the connective biology. On top of this, the stepmother is experiencing heavy guilt about her negative feelings toward the dad and his kids. This isn't what she signed up for.

The problem here is that the adults in this blending family entered into marriage with the idea of behaving like a first-marriage family. The dad is enjoying the idea that the stepmom will assume the responsibilities for his children like a bio-mom would. *But her emotional energy will quickly drain because she is not the biological mother!* This attitude of acting like a couple in a first marriage is causing major conflict, unnecessary guilt, and a great deal of unhappiness.

Sustaining the stepparent

Parents can go the distance with their own children and can do so indefinitely. Their shared nuclear bonds enable them to endure just about anything. They pay out untold amounts of money and work day and night for their own kids for years—and do so without ceremony, thanks, or appreciation from anyone.

But this is not the world of the stepparent. Lacking a nuclear connection, it is extremely difficult to undergo constant obligations to somebody else's kids. Many cannot endure.

The only thing that will give stepparents the energy and motivation to stay involved with their stepchildren over time, particularly difficult stepchildren, is recognition and appreciation for their selfless efforts by the parent. Follow the model of grandparents, who in most cases receive lots of praise and thanks for their efforts.

It is the biological parent who must become the stepparent's biggest cheerleader. Requiring thanks and appreciation from the children is a hopeless task. What will not come from the children must come from the parent. It's the biological parent who needs to say to the stepparent, "I just want you to know that I'm aware of all that you are doing for my kids, and I want to tell you how much I appreciate your help and effort. Making the kids' lunches this morning and taking Robin to practice this afternoon really helped and was wonderful of you. Thank you so much."

It's amazing what stepparents will endure if parents lavish recognition and praise on them.

It comes down to this: The blending family will experience relief and stability never before experienced if parents accept the reality of the step-connections *as step-connections* and continue to be responsible for their own kids, showering praise on their spouses for lending a hand.

Acts of kindness toward all stepchildren

The feelings stepparents have toward their stepchildren are what they are, and need to be accepted. Stepparents may end up loving their stepchildren or outright disliking them—or land somewhere in between. Parents must allow stepparents to work out their own feelings toward the stepchildren.

Some children are very easygoing and easy to love; others are difficult to be around. Sometimes the nuclear bonds remain quiet and relationships are easy; other times the bonds remain awake, keeping everyone at arm's length. This is just the reality of how things go in a blending family.

Yet, regardless of how stepparents feel toward the stepchildren, what is required of every stepparent is acts of kindness and caring toward all of them.

Because feelings change, stepparents cannot act on how they feel. What is required in stepparenting is to maintain a caring environment in which all of the children feel loved and supported.

We think every bio-parent should say the following to the stepparent:

- I will accept full responsibility for my own children.
- I will welcome you as a parent to my children, but I will be mindful that you are doing so willingly, without obligation.
- For my children's sake and for our family's sake, I will do my utmost to build a peaceful relationship with my children's other parent and partner.
- I will teach my children to be courteous and respectful toward you.
- To make things easier for you, I will teach my children to have good personal habits.
- I will also teach my children to clean up after themselves.
- As you do things for my children, I will regularly communicate my appreciation to you.
- You have the freedom to develop your own level of feelings toward my children.

And the following should be said to every parent by the stepparent:

- I will always act in a caring and kind manner toward your children.
- I will join with you in building a peaceful and good relationship with your former spouse and his (her) partner.

- I will encourage you and give you my full support when you wish to be with your children, either with me or without me.

~

Making Your Blending Family Work

Parents bear the responsibility for their own children, not stepparents.

The stepparent should receive thanks and recognition from the parent for any service or kindness to the parent's children.

7

THE AUTHORITY OF THE BIOLOGICAL PARENT IN DISCIPLINE

Accepting the Discipline Process

W hat are stepparents to do if the stepchildren's behavior is out of hand and the biological parents refuse to or are somehow incapable of disciplining the children? Are stepparents supposed to stand by helplessly and do nothing while the stepchildren become little tyrants in the family? Are they to allow the obnoxious behavior of their stepchildren to influence their own kids?

When a parent fails to discipline, it is sometimes possible for the stepparent to take action to remedy the problem. We know of many instances in which stepparents have spent long hours successfully tutoring their stepchildren, coaching and counseling them, and enforcing strict rules and boundaries. The goal in a stepfamily would be that *both* parents *and* stepparents can discipline and apply controls to *all* of the children.

We encourage all stepparents to roll up their sleeves and get involved in their stepchildren's lives—to the degree that it works.

But when the stepparent's efforts cease to work and when more attempts at discipline will become hurtful to the relationship, the stepparent must quit. Unlike the bio parents, who can continue to discipline even though a child is strongly resistant, stepparents cannot.

When the child berates the stepparent or when the stepparent becomes the focus of ridicule and disrespect, the efforts of the stepparent have ceased to be effective. It's time for the stepparent to close down any attempts at parenting. Once such emotions and behaviors arise on the part of the child, the stepparent must stop. Stepparents cannot force discipline on a hostile stepchild. In contrast to a parent's discipline, which rarely causes permanent relational damage, unwanted discipline by stepparents can severely damage their relationship with the stepchild.

Stepparents are prisoners in their own homes

All too frequently, stepparents feel as if they are prisoners in their own home.

They are frustrated when their desires and wants are ignored and attention is focused on a self-centered stepkid. They resent the disrespect shown them by the kids and the parent. Yet, it seems that stepparents are supposed to endure the misery, accept the rude behavior, pay the money, and submit without complaint to, in their opinion, parent/child dysfunction. On top of all this, the stepparent sees that things are going from bad to worse and is prevented from undertaking any course of correction.

Isn't marriage a team effort? Don't both adults have a voice? Don't the words of a stepparent count? Are stepparents supposed to just stand by and be held hostage to the inability of a parent to act like a parent and the resulting rude and undisciplined behavior of a stepchild? And why are some parents so blindly supportive of their out-of-control child and disrespectful of the desires of the stepparent? Under these extreme circumstances shouldn't stepparents just seize control and force some sense and stability into the family?

The poor stepparents. Some live with spouses driven by guilt, seeking to buy the children's favor and forgiveness due to a past divorce. Other spouses are terrified that, if disciplined, the children will withdraw their affection and favor their other parent. And sometimes stepparents have to just watch and endure lousy parenting skills—to everyone's deep misery and the harm of the children.

What is a stepparent to do?

The fact is marriage *is* a team effort. And yes, stepparents *should* have a voice. Stepparents should not be held prisoner in their own homes by an incompetent parent and/or an unmanageable child.

But, unhappily for some, the reality is that stepparents are under the control of the parents. At any moment it's the parent who can support or demolish stepparent authority. This includes not only the parent in the home but the child's other parent who may be encouraging the kid to ignore the stepparent.

There are a number of solutions that work and we offer five. Nobody's saying these solutions are easy but they are effective. Here they are in brief:

1. **Don't sweat the small stuff.** Stepparents have to let a lot of things go.

2. **Consult a third party.** Be sure the third party individual is part of a good working blending family. First-marriage adults usually don't get it.

3. If the parent is unwilling or incapable of managing the child and you are powerless to help, a very effective solution is to allow the child to experience failure. This is a long-term solution but is very, very effective. Continual suffering usually brings maturity.

4. If you can't control your stepchildren, you can still control your own. Don't hesitate to set up separate rules for your own children.

5. If you feel unsafe living with an unmanageable teenager or adult child, take your children and leave the household, living elsewhere until the child is older and independent of the family. You are separating from the child, not your spouse, but for your peace of mind you need to live in a separate place.

1. Don't sweat the small stuff

One parent complained to me that his wife's two boys were taking advantage of their mother by being allowed to use her car any time they asked for it. The stepparent thought that the boys should learn to walk or ride their bikes or take public transportation. I asked the stepdad and mother, "Are the kids good kids? Are they doing okay in school, do they have good friends, do they pitch in and do their chores around the home?" After affirmative answers from the mother and stepparent I told the stepparent to leave well enough alone. The mother and her boys had worked out a pattern in their lives and the car issue wasn't important to anyone except the stepparent. The stepparent should not create a problem where there wasn't one. He needed to back off.

Even though the kids are doing okay in school, have respectable friends, and act decently at home, blending parents continue to clash over parenting styles. Some disagreements may be as minor as kids leaving a light on in their bedroom or abandoning sports equipment in the driveway. Such minor infractions should never become a big deal.

When parents discuss issues like these, words like, "disrespect, lack of consideration, disobedience, self-centered, selfishness," should never be used. Keep small issues small. All kids leave bikes on driveways and lights on in the house. Enjoy the kids!

In our own stepfamily I had a problem with my young stepson, Matt. His table manners were, to me, awful. He was a happy and good kid, but his mother allowed him to be sloppy at the table. One time I asked Matt to notice how the other kids ate their meals—they didn't spill food everywhere the way Matt did. But my attempt at correction went completely over his head.

The issue could have escalated, but I forced myself to make it a non-issue. Matt's mom didn't seem to think it was important, and I'm relieved that I didn't, either.

It wasn't funny then, but it's funny now. When we as a family ever refer to this subject, we all laugh over Matt's table manners as a young child. Twenty years later I'm here to say that Matt has turned out just fine. Over the years the childhood problem disappeared, and today Matt is married, well-mannered and has excellent eating habits.

People may not remember what you say to them, but they will remember how you make them feel. As I look back, I'm extremely pleased that I forced myself to drop the issue of Matt's eating habits because today he has only fond thoughts about me—but I could have ruined our relationship over something as insignificant as how he held his fork.

As Jenetha and I look back over the years, all the issues we thought were so important to correct about each other's children have vanished.

An important difference between parents and stepparents

With our own kids we are forever tolerant—it's built-in and automatic. But as stepparents, we magnify the trespasses of our stepchildren and stress the need for stricter guidelines and punishments. Tolerance of stepparents toward stepchildren is not automatic and must be learned and practiced.

As a stepparent you should repeatedly tell yourself, "I tend to be harder on my stepchildren," and then back off. You should think to yourself, "He's just a young kid, or she's just a struggling teenager," recognizing that kids will always say and do dumb things.

When you marry an adult with children, you take on the entire family. You have just accepted a complete mature family into your life, a family composed of good things but also problems and difficulties. Accepting just the good parts of the family and not the deficiencies and challenges is unwise and harmful to the health of your blending family.

"You mean I have to accept his daughter's rude and caustic attitudes?" In a sense, yes! Remember the awakened bonds. A blending family is healthy when all of the good and bad in each family member is accepted and embraced. To just accept the good and immediately try to rid the new family of unwanted difficulties is harmful. Family members won't tolerate you trying to make changes, and you will be rejected.

Acceptance is stability. Acceptance is when you as a stepparent communicate to your non-biological family members that you're not going anywhere, that you are committed to the family, that your love for your family is greater than these issues, that you'll do whatever is necessary to resolve problems and repair family difficulties.

When joining together each adult will want to fully embrace the other family, accepting all the good and all the bad and allowing time and caring correction to bring the family to health and stability.

2. Consult a third party advocate

What is a stepparent to do if the biological parent refuses to control the children when the issues are not minor? We're talking about problems like failing in school, negative attitudes toward adults, recreational alcohol and drug use, immorality, or obnoxious personal habits.

In one family, a parent allowed his son to stay out at night until all hours. The parent knew that his son was probably out drinking, yet he would neither restrict the boy nor see to it that he was home at a decent hour. Another parent was aware that her daughter was sexually active with her boyfriend but wouldn't take measures to block the relationship. And then there's the parent who realized that her son was failing in school but wouldn't spend the time or energy to help the boy bring up his grades. The boy rejected efforts of help from his stepdad.

What are you, the stepparent, to do? You are witnessing the failure of your stepchild at the hand of the parent and are powerless to help.

One option is to try a third party. Find another stepfamily who has successfully worked through the same issues. Ask their help. Seek their advice. Hopefully the third-party approach will convince the parent to utilize an alternative approach to child-raising.

If a third party advocate doesn't work, try to take (not send) the parent to counseling or parenting classes. Speak with church clergy and enlist their prayers and help. Join a prayer group, hopefully with the parent. Is the child's other parent available to step in and help? Look to involving school counselors, social services, drug rehabilitation services, or police.

3. Allow the child to experience failure

If you have no control, and the parent is unwilling or incapable of working with the child, there remains another powerful option for you, the stepparent: letting the parent and child experience failure.

Failure can be, and is, an extremely good instructional tool. Letting the parent suffer the results of mismanagement and the child suffer the results of misbehavior is a valid parenting strategy and may be the only corrective tool available.

Remember the story of the prodigal son?[1] Jesus told of a young man who took an early inheritance from his father and left his father and brother to live a life of his own choosing. In asking for an early inheritance the son in so many words told his father and brother that he wanted no more to do with them. The father, knowing there was nothing he could do to change his son's mind, gave him his inheritance. He knew the only solution was for his son to learn the hard way: to make mistakes, to suffer the consequences, and to hopefully learn and grow up.

The principle for stepfamilies is this: If stepparents are prevented from making any corrections, then they must let the parent and child experience the results of their own behavior choices.

Failure can be a great instructor. Letting a child fail means that the stepparent ceases any further discipline or correction of the child. The stepparent releases the child and child's parent into God's hands. The stepparent then ceases to be an agent of correction and is never again critical or angry at the child or parent over this issue.

How to release a child to God

Allowing a child to experience failure doesn't mean that the stepparent gives up on the child. The stepparent is using an effective parenting strategy when there seems to be nothing else to do—the same strategy the father used in the story of the prodigal son.

And like the father of the prodigal son, the stepparent remains willing and ready to lend assistance if asked.

One stepparent told her husband and stepson that she had done all she could to help raise the boy but felt snubbed and ignored at every turn. She knows that because of the boy's undisciplined behaviors he is certain to experience some tragedy and failure in the future. Yet, any further correction by her was working against her relationship with the boy and causing serious problems in her marriage. So, the mother backed off.

Here are some things you can say to your spouse when you back away:

"You know what I think about how you're raising your child. So I'm going to stop arguing and let you do what seems best."

"It must be difficult for you, having your ex-spouse and me always telling you what to do about your kids. No matter what you do, you always seem to get criticized. I don't want to be part of the problem any longer."

"I do not fully understand the decisions you are making for your children. But you are the parent, and I'm going to back off and let you handle your kids your way."

"I want you to know that even though I disagree with your rules, I'm with you, I support you, and I will accept your decisions about how to raise your own children."

Even though you may not *feel* like being encouraging and supportive, support the parent anyway! Make yourself influential by being the first to let go. Pray for your spouse and stepchildren. Be a friend to both. Be loving and kind. Be encouraging. Don't be afraid to let failure happen. But be ready to give assistance when the children fail and you are called upon to help.

4. Set up separate rules in your household

What if spouses won't correct their own children and the children start to have a bad influence on the stepparents' kids?

In one blending family the eldest daughter's interest in music and friends turned counterculture. Pleas for help by the stepmom and demands for discipline went unheeded by the father. And what was most troubling was that the older girl was beginning to influence the stepmother's own 10-year-old daughter.

This put the stepmother in a very difficult situation. Since her husband refused to control his own daughter, the stepmother was forced to create separate rules for her child.

In blending families, separate rules are more common than you might think.

Parents never have to allow their children to do things of which they don't approve. The stepmother in this story simply explained to her daughter that she did not approve of her older (step)sister's friends, their appearance, or their music. She told her daughter that she would not be allowed to imitate their behavior or to join her stepsister in any of these activities. This meant, pretty much, that her stepsister's bedroom and her music and her friends were off limits to the 10-year-old.

We know of many stepfamilies with separate rules of conduct for their kids, and, after a while, the rules become second nature. All of the blending family members know that in *this* family, in *this* house, *these* are the rules.

This situation actually took place in our own household. Jenetha allowed her daughter freedoms that I disagreed with. I felt that while her daughter was living in our home, she should follow certain rules. Jenetha disagreed and allowed her daughter to continue to enjoy certain freedoms. Since this was her daughter, I backed off. I had said what I felt I needed to say, so I dropped the subject. For the next year and a half I kept quiet about the matter. I did tell *my* younger daughter, however, that when she was older she was not to expect the same freedoms.

Understand the climate of your family

Your ability to discipline your stepchildren will ebb and flow. One day the stepchildren will allow you full rights in discipline and correction. The next day the positive emotional climate has disappeared and the stepchildren are hostile to any of your correctives.

You must be sensitive to the climate of your blending family before attempting any discipline. If the climate is peaceful, you can exercise full parenting rights, including discipline. If the climate is tenuous, you will be wise to back off and let the parent perform any correction or discipline.

If the climate is not favorable, and you try to force discipline anyway, you will only awaken the nuclear bonds, which will prove to be extremely hazardous to the entire blending family. Parenting in blending families is not like parenting in first marriages in which everyone shares the same nuclear bonds. With separate nuclear bonds, when the climate isn't favorable to discipline and it's forced on the children anyway, nuclear bonds will go to war.

5. Separate from an unsafe household

What if a stepchild gets out of control and becomes involved in criminal behavior?

Here is the way one blending family handled a problem with the husband's older teenage son. Prior to their marriage, as a way to help the troubled son, his grandparents had offered to let him come and live on their farm. Two years later, the son became more than the grandparents could handle. Following some trouble with the law, the grandparents sent their grandson back to live with his father.

During the two years the boy was living with his grandparents the father had married a woman with two young children. Shortly after the boy joined the family, some events occurred that caused the stepmother to fear for the safety of herself and her children. She told her husband that the son could no longer live in their home.

Knowing that the husband must care for his son, the couple agreed that the dad and son would live separately from the rest of the family. The marriage continued, but in two separate households. The new family structure insured that the wife and children would never have to be alone with the boy without the father present. This arrangement continued until the boy moved out on his own.

What made this blending family work was the couple's sincere understanding and acceptance of the nuclear bond. They knew that the boy's future depended on his father's attention, loyalty, and support. Because of her acceptance of the bond, the wife didn't force her husband to choose between his son and her. She didn't ask her husband to reject his son, nor was she willing to discard the marriage. What would normally have ended a marriage actually strengthened the relationship of this couple.

Was the stepmother right to refuse to let her stepson live in her home? Absolutely! Was the stepmother violating the principle that all nuclear bonds must be accepted? Absolutely not! In fact, in having the father move out to be with his son—without ending the marriage, the couple reinforced the principle. The stepmother was right in trying to protect herself and her children. Accepting bonds never suggests that parents should put themselves or their children in danger.

Accepting bonds does suggest that couples do what it takes, even to the point of causing their own marriage some discomfort, to support parents with especially difficult children.

Making Your Blending Family Work

Five responses by stepparents to parents who will not *discipline their kids and prevent you from making corrections:*

1. Let the small stuff go.

2. Find a third party arbitrator.

3. Understand that part of parenting may be allowing a child to experience failure.

4. If your spouse's kids are having a negative influence on your children, lay down separate rules.

5. If a situation becomes truly harmful or threatening, remove yourself and your children.

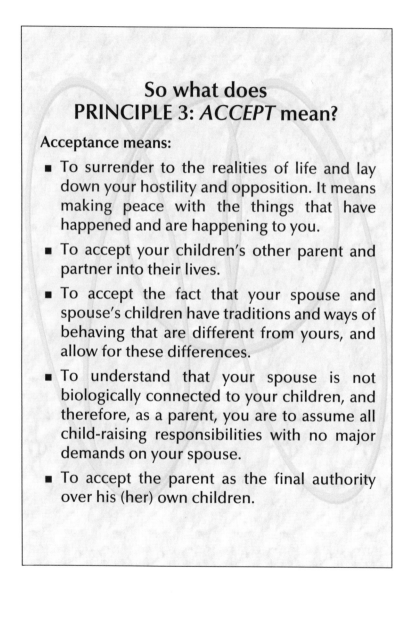

So what does
PRINCIPLE 3: *ACCEPT* mean?

Acceptance means:

- To surrender to the realities of life and lay down your hostility and opposition. It means making peace with the things that have happened and are happening to you.

- To accept your children's other parent and partner into their lives.

- To accept the fact that your spouse and spouse's children have traditions and ways of behaving that are different from yours, and allow for these differences.

- To understand that your spouse is not biologically connected to your children, and therefore, as a parent, you are to assume all child-raising responsibilities with no major demands on your spouse.

- To accept the parent as the final authority over his (her) own children.

Principle 4

SEPARATE

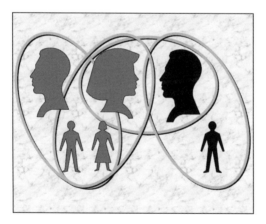

8

LETTING YOUR EX LIVE HIS (HER) OWN LIFE

Separating from All Outside Bonds and Connections

Separating from outside bonds

Separating from bonds and step-connections is the fourth principle in the art of making blending families work.

Because nuclear bonds resist overlapping or merging, it's important to distance yourself from all the nuclear bonds that are outside your family. An outside bond is the bond your children have with their other parent and an outside step-connection is their connection with the other parent's partner. Separating nuclear bonds means that you do not interfere with the other parents or step-parents, the individuals who are connected to your kids but outside your personal bonds.

Whenever outside bonds overlap—when one parent tries to dictate instructions to the other parent or interfere with the function of the other family—there is always conflict. Therefore, in order to create a healthy blending family, you have to *separate from all bonds and connections that are not part of your immediate blending family.*

What to do with Tina's family

Remember Tina and her husband Brett in Chapter 3? At the end of that chapter we sketched out her family, and just for fun asked you to try to figure out all of her family's bonds and step-connections. We found that her stepfamily has twenty-one separate connections, six inside the family and fifteen outside. Any one of the fifteen outside relationships has the potential to spell disaster. For their family's survival and sanity, Tina and Brett will have to severely limit their involvement and concerns with those outside relationships.

The fifteen outside bonds and step-connections may be permanent fixtures and ever present in the lives of Tina and Brett. Yet, they don't have to be a burden on the couple or their family. Tina and Brett's goals are to keep from involving themselves in the lives of their former spouses and not let the other adults become involved in theirs. If the families can remain separate and allow members to co-exist peacefully, the families will be a lot more manageable. The expenditure of time and energy by the parents must be focused on what goes on in their own household.

Remember, we are talking about the parents, not the children. What the parents must separate from, the children cannot and must not. What are *outside* bonds to Tina and her husband are *inside* bonds and connections to their children. What is not family to Tina is family to her children. The kids must remain connected to their other families, but the parents must separate *themselves* from the other families.

A family in crisis: Tina

Tina is industrious and highly responsible and the self-appointed administrator of the family. To Tina, this means making suggestions and recommendations to the children's other parents and stepparents, persons outside of her bonds.

Tina's involvement in everyone's life is creating major problems. What Tina views as responsible and caring interaction, the other parents consider intrusion and attempts at domination and control. When Tina's children travel to their other parent's home, Tina calls to inform the other parents about the children's homework assignments and sports schedules. She then follows up to check on whether her daughter has done her homework or to leave messages reminding her former husband of their son's dental appointments. The other parents are getting more and more exasperated with her constant intrusion into their private time with their kids.

Tina's ex-husband has finally had enough and told Tina that when his daughter arrives at his house, he will keep her cell phone and return it to her when Tina picks her up. It is clear to him that his daughter cannot settle in mentally or emotionally at his house with a constant barrage of phone calls from her mom.

Everyone is beginning to hate Tina's interference, even Tina's kids and stepchildren. By her meddling actions, Tina is creating a great deal of animosity between herself and other family members.

For Tina to restore relationships and bring about peace, she will have to limit herself to managing her own home. She has six bonds and step-connections to deal with in her own family, which is a lifetime of work in itself. Tina needs to oversee just her own family *during the time they are in her home.* When Tina's kids and stepkids go off to their other homes, she needs to let go and allow the other parents to raise the children without interference.

This is the case for all parents, even parents with young children. Parents must resist trying to manage the children when they are with their other parents.

Lack of involvement does not mean lack of awareness

Certainly, good parenting means being aware always of what is taking place in the other household.

In our own blending family, Jenetha and I were very conscious of what went on in the children's other homes. We think every parent should be. But we tried always to remain uninvolved and not intrude into the kids' lives when they were with their other parents.

Years ago I once crossed the line and tried to instruct my children's mother and stepfather about better methods of parenting. To this day I regret my actions. The children suffered terribly. I awoke the nuclear bonds, and the war that ensued was horrific.

If our children had ever been in physical danger, we would immediately have taken some action—but this was not the case. Still, it was sometimes hard for us not to make some suggestions when we disapproved of how our children were being raised in their other homes—and, most likely, the other parents probably felt the same way towards us. Fortunately for everyone, we all remained detached and let each family choose their own style of parenting.

Brett, Tina's husband, has his own struggles with separating from outside bonds. Whenever his ex-wife calls with a household problem, Brett drops everything and runs right over. He likes helping out his former spouse, but it's making Tina miserable. She is disturbed by Brett's eagerness to assist his ex-wife. The next time there's a leaky faucet Tina wants Brett to tell his ex-wife to call a plumber.

Brett insists that he's trying to keep on good terms with his ex-wife for the benefit of his kids. For their sake, he says, he wants to stay on her good side. However, Tina doesn't buy this explanation. She believes that the ex-wife is still emotionally connected to Brett and uses home maintenance as an excuse to get him to come over. Tina also suspects that Brett's lack of boundaries with his ex-wife is causing his daughters to wonder if their dad and mom might get back together.

To Brett's way of thinking, he's behaving responsibly. He is keeping a good relationship going with his ex, he is staying more in touch with his kids, he's modeling good parenting, and he's making a positive difference in the kids' other household. Other than the fact that Tina doesn't like what he's doing, what can possibly be the problem?

The problem is that Brett's actions are becoming toxic to both families. They are affecting his marriage with Tina and are causing the daughters to withdraw emotionally from Tina. This is the main reason his kids disrespect Tina. They secretly believe that Tina is on her way out.

Successful separation

Brett's behavior is causing lots of confusion for everyone. For the emotional health and stability of all involved, Brett must not go into his ex-wife's house any more. He needs to remain on good terms with his former wife, but he has to stop rescuing her. He needs to focus on his own family, and the ex-wife needs to learn to live independently from Brett. Tina is right. If a faucet needs fixing, his ex-wife should call a plumber.

Separating yourself, not your kids!

Even though nuclear bonds require former partners to separate from each other, the same bonds require the children to do the exact opposite. The very bonds that require *separation* of the parents *join* the children. Children need full emotional integration into both biological bonds with both parents and stepparents in both families.

If the other parent displays some areas of irresponsibility, and you've tried your best to work things out, but the other parent refuses to cooperate, you'll have to make up the difference. Forget trying to change the other parent. Fill in where the other parent lacks.

Maintaining boundaries

Separating from bonds and connections also means not allowing family privileges for persons outside your family. Brett does not have the right to walk into his ex-spouse's home, sit wherever he chooses, or freely walk around the home. He cannot act as if he is part of the other family. This means that Brett may not exercise any privileges at his ex-wife's home, even though his ex-wife welcomes him. Parents must not share in the same exclusive privileges that their children have at their other household.

Brett needs to treat his ex-wife the way he treats a neighbor. He needs to be friendly but respectful of his neighbor's personal space, and leave the responsibility for all the neighbor's maintenance and repairs to his neighbor.

Helping your kids connect emotionally with their other household

When children are on weekend visits at the other household, you should rarely, if ever, intrude in any way, including trying to call them. Children need the entire weekend to settle into the other home. Constant or lengthy conversations prevent full transition.

Parents who do not have primary custody and see their children infrequently are encouraged to have open communication with their children, yet remain as non-intrusive and respectful of the other household as possible. Both sides need to work together to agree on the best times to have extended phone conversations. For their emotional health, children need to have full connections with both households.

When ending phone conversations with your children, try to help them transition emotionally away from you and back to the other parent. End your calls by giving your children the gift of the other family. Telling your kids you miss them and are lonely without them and then hanging up is very hard on them. Rather, at the end of a conversation, say something positive about the child's mom or dad and the stepparent. Be upbeat. Don't say, "I miss you. Good bye." Say, "We'll talk right after you get back. Have a great weekend with your mom and Dave."

Protecting your kids

If parents suspect problems at the other household that might cause physical or emotional injury to their children, they are under obligation to remove the children from the unsafe environment. Parents have absolute rights at all times to protect their children.

However, because of the high level of emotion that exists between most separated parents, what may qualify as an unsafe or abusive environment is sometimes open to interpretation. Animosity creates suspicion and accusation. We've known parents to accuse the other parent of abuse because the kids were fed fast-food. We've heard parents claim abuse because the other parents required their children to attend church—or not to attend church—and the list goes on and on.

If one former spouse suspects the other of abuse, impartial professionals need to be consulted immediately. Professionals can help you determine whether or not your children are in an unsafe environment and offer you substantial advice.

─────────────── ⌇ ───────────────

Making Your Blending Family Work

When adults separate from outside bonds and step-connections, families can experience peace.

9

GIVING FREEDOM TO THE PARENT/CHILD RELATIONSHIP

On Occasion, Separating from Inside Connections

Strange as it may seem, sometimes stepparents have to separate from bonds *inside* the blending family. Raising healthy children may mean that a stepparent, by agreement, needs to retreat and give the biological parent and child time to sort things out just between themselves.

Nuclear war

Al has always had a difficult relationship with his ex-wife. The woman is extremely hostile to him and has succeeded in turning his two daughters against him. And unfortunately, since Al's recent marriage to Kathy, Al was not surprised to learn that his new wife is also held in disdain by his ex-wife and daughters.

Kathy and Al live in Al's home; and whatever Kathy does to the house, whether she replaces a carpet or adds some furniture, the daughters ridicule her. They also criticize Kathy's cooking and the way she dresses, and refuse to answer when she attempts to talk to them.

Kathy has been very hurt by these girls and has asked Al to discipline them, to put an immediate stop to their rude and offensive behavior. Yet Al knows that if he attempts to discipline his daughters, they will simply stop coming over to his house (something quite acceptable to Kathy). Al desires to hang on to his relationship with his daughters, minimal as it is, by ignoring their obnoxious behavior.

Things have become so difficult between the daughters and stepmother that they told their father that if he wished to see them again he would have to do so without Kathy present. To Kathy's horror, Al agreed.

Kathy feels that Al is dishonoring their marriage by agreeing to his daughters' demands. She feels that if you get Al, you get her, too! If the daughters cannot abide by these simple terms, then their father is not available.

Al does not want to cause any more damage to his already tenuous relationship with his daughters. He hopes the time will come when he can include Kathy on future visits with the children, but for now he is willing to leave Kathy behind if that is what it takes for him to be with his kids. He wants Kathy to allow him to see his daughters without making a big deal out of the whole thing.

As it stands now, Kathy has flatly refused to go along with Al's wishes. To her, she and Al are a team, and Al should make a stand for their marriage. But Al remains committed to his daughters, whatever it takes. Kathy and Al have reached an impasse, and neither will budge.

What happened?

What happened is that Kathy married into a relationship with highly awakened nuclear bonds. The bonds were already at work creating opposition between Al and his ex-wife and daughters long before Kathy entered the picture. What made everything worse is that Kathy entered into this nuclear war with an awakened nuclear bond of her own. Kathy's bond with her new husband threw her into immediate action to protect her marriage and repel the ex-wife and daughters.

These family members are now participants in an all-out war. Kathy feels that if the daughters continue to be rude and unmanageable, they will never be welcome in her home again. Since she has no bond with the daughters, she can easily write them off in favor of her marriage to their father.

The feeling is mutual with the daughters and the mother. Trained by the mother to believe that Kathy has taken their father away from them, the daughters wouldn't mind if they never saw her again. And the mother feels victorious in having caused disruption in Al's life and having the daughters on her side.

The person most miserable in this big mess is Al, who so strongly desires a peaceful and loving relationship with his new wife and with his two daughters, but at this point has neither.

The solution

Al and Kathy's absolute first goal in their marriage is to support and strengthen Al's relationship with his daughters. Kathy is an adult, a strong capable woman, and can take the heat. The daughters cannot. They are children. They are dependent, young, irresponsible, and needy. They are pawns in a battle—victims involving forces and broken relationships beyond their control. Never should any lines be drawn between a parent and a dependent child. Al and his daughters share the same DNA, they are one person, and he cannot be asked to draw a line down the middle of himself.

Any solution that fosters a separation of parent and child is not viable.

What must not happen is separation between the father and the children. Al must fulfill his role as a father. His daughters don't know it, but they badly need him. Their appalling behavior only confirms the fact that they need their father more than ever.

Al cannot back away. He's right. Whatever it takes and whatever conditions are required, he must continue to see his daughters and try to build a solid relationship with them. He must not agree to Kathy's demand to back away from his children just because they are difficult and critical of him and Kathy.

Kathy is the one who should back off. *She must not use the sacredness of her marriage as a tool for injury.* She needs to continue to love Al and support their marriage, but also to separate herself from this difficult issue and let Al be a dad to his kids.

During this crucial time, Kathy needs to be *agreeable* to whatever Al thinks is necessary to restore his daughters to him. *Encouraged* by Kathy, Al needs to be free to spend extra time with his children.

This is not to say that Al's daughters don't need to be disciplined. They need discipline big time! Their anger, rudeness, and disrespectful behavior will only bring harm to themselves, and they need immediate and stern correction. But right now Al can do little to change anything. His kids are living with their mother and are out from under his influence. Plus, the girls' mother supports their decision to despise Kathy and disrespect their father. So to try to discipline them would be fruitless and would only cause more anguish for everyone concerned.

Establishing a closer relationship with his two children will have to *precede* any attempts by Al to discipline them. Discipline may follow eventually, but only after a long period of rebuilding on the part of their father.[1]

But Al and Kathy are a team.
Aren't they supposed to act as a team?

This isn't a first marriage in which everyone belongs to the same family and has the same biology. There are powers and forces and agendas and struggles going on that must be identified, accepted, and dealt with wisely. If Al and Kathy try to bully their way through, forget about nuclear bonds, and disregard the power of the bonds, Al's relationship with his children will be damaged for decades to come. And the emotional damage to the daughters will be catastrophic.

The marriage relationship cannot be used as a tool for harm. Forcing overlapping bonds and step-connections at this time, under the volatile emotional climate in Al's family, will prove extremely harmful to the family.

For Al to be with his children without Kathy is not, and should not be, harmful to his marriage. The exact opposite! It should ultimately help to restore the family. Al must be allowed to invest in his damaged relationship with his kids now, with the hope of restoring it. He needs to begin first to repair his own relationship with his children, and then slowly reintroduce Kathy back into his daughters' lives.

Kathy's first response to being considered an outsider to Al and his children may be to feel threatened or abandoned. However, she can't allow herself to feel slighted, or in competition with Al's children, or that Al's children are "winning." Kathy must *give Al to his kids* in order for him to fulfill his responsibility as a parent.

In backing away, Kathy still can do things to build her blending family. She can let Al be with his children without giving him a hard time. She can be her husband's best fan, encouraging him to take time to be alone with his kids. She can be ready to welcome the girls back into her home when they are willing to come.

If Kathy can learn to display these attitudes, she will enjoy tremendous benefit in a happy marriage to Al and a wonderful future relationship with his kids.

The power of humility and love

Let's take the worst scenario. Let's say you're in a situation like Al and Kathy's and you, the stepmother, have tried to adapt to your difficult situation. It's a year later, and nothing has changed. The children still only want to see their dad and will not tolerate being in the same room with you. What are you to do?

If children *never* accept a parent or stepparent, and if they continue to be rude, bad-mannered, and spiteful toward their parent or stepparent, *you must continue to give unconditional support to your spouse in caring for his kids.*

In rare circumstances parents may have to put space between themselves and an adult child as a protection from harm or abuse. But even from a distance, parents must remain loyal and loving toward their children.

A parent's unconditional love can reach beyond behavior, rules, and personal character into the depths of the life of a child. It is this love, implanted deep within, that can bring a child back into a world of wholeness and responsibility and right behavior. It may take years before the child finally matures. It may never happen. But it *can* happen.

———————————— ∾ ————————————

Making Your Blending Family Work

At times, stepparents may need to retreat and let parents rebuild a relationship with their own children.

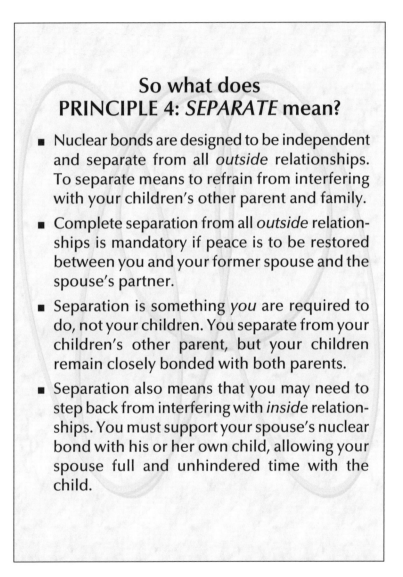

So what does PRINCIPLE 4: *SEPARATE* mean?

- Nuclear bonds are designed to be independent and separate from all *outside* relationships. To separate means to refrain from interfering with your children's other parent and family.

- Complete separation from all *outside* relationships is mandatory if peace is to be restored between you and your former spouse and the spouse's partner.

- Separation is something *you* are required to do, not your children. You separate from your children's other parent, but your children remain closely bonded with both parents.

- Separation also means that you may need to step back from interfering with *inside* relationships. You must support your spouse's nuclear bond with his or her own child, allowing your spouse full and unhindered time with the child.

Principle 5

BENEFIT

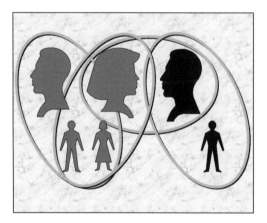

10

MAKING PEACE WITH YOUR EX AND YOUR EX'S PARTNER

Benefiting All Outside Bonds and Connections

Benefiting bonds and step-connections is the fifth and final principle in the art of keeping nuclear bonds quiet and building a successful stepfamily. When you practice this final principle, the nuclear bonds that are not designed to overlap, and the step-connections that are generally hotbeds of trouble, can co-exist peaceably. With quiet bonds yours will be a peaceful home.

The fifth principle is the most rewarding and most powerful of all the principles and will do more to keep nuclear bonds quiet than any other, allowing your family to attain even deeper levels of satisfaction. However, we need to say that this fifth principle is sometimes the most difficult to learn and to do.

Benefiting bonds and step-connections means to move beyond an attitude of acceptance to actually performing *acts of kindness* for all of your various bonds and connections. Benefiting *outside* bonds, the focus of this chapter, means to look for opportunities to bless or to do special favors for your children's other family members.

Making peace

Jesus said, *Blessed are the peacemakers, for they shall be called sons of God.*[1] What Jesus did not say is, "Blessed are those who want peace," or, "Blessed are those who are peaceful," although we know that these are excellent traits. Jesus specifically said that it is the peace*makers*, those who *make* peace, who have the high honor of being known as children of God.

A soft answer turns away wrath, but a harsh word stirs up anger.[2] The amazing thing about this proverb is that it not only describes how to calm wrath or fuel a fire, it also indicates that you can influence others. By acting in certain ways, you can actually control the emotions and actions of other people. It is one example of how to be a peace-*maker!*

With all of the bonds and step-connections in and around your family, there are bound to be some major conflicts. It's inevitable. The way to transform war into peace and create workable relationships is for you to begin a chain reaction of calm, non-reactive, complimentary behavior. It is in your hands to *make* peace among your family members. Don't wait for somebody else to make the move. Be that person. Begin now.

Granddad Paul as the peace*maker*

Paul is the father of Jenetha's ex-husband and the grandfather of my stepchildren. Throughout the years I had seen him at special occasions like my stepchildren's birthdays and graduations. He was always pleasant and talkative, but I found myself holding him at arm's length. He was my wife's former husband's father, for goodness sake! What relationship could we ever have?

At one of these events, Paul asked me about my son, Dustin, who was playing baseball in high school. Paul had heard that Dustin had received a letter of interest to play at the University of Arizona. He asked me about Dustin's prospects, and then the conversation became so much more than that.

"Don, you know I live in the Scottsdale area, not far from the University of Arizona," Paul said to me. "If Dustin were to play baseball there, I'd be his number one fan. I'd attend every one of his games."

I stood amazed. Why would the father of my wife's ex-husband be so generous of his time for my son? Aren't divorced family members supposed to create a "you are separate from us" atmosphere?

Not according to Paul. Paul was reaching beyond his own family to the "other side." His thoughtfulness and ease at ignoring bonded lines amazed me.

And Paul's interest wasn't just in Dustin. He wanted to know about my entire family—he wanted to learn everyone's names and was interested in all of our activities. It was as if this gentleman had developed an acute case of amnesia. He acted as if there were no lines drawn in the sand, as if there were no difficulties between former family members.

When a divorce occurs, everyone in the family suffers some heartbreaking and troubling times. But Paul turned what was emotionally very difficult for him—the break-up of the marriage of his son and daughter-in-law—into an opportunity to meet and care for a new marriage partner and new family members.

Just look at what Granddad Paul did to me! In being sincerely interested in my son, Granddad Paul made me like him. When Paul complimented my son, he disarmed me.

We're saying to you that it *is* possible to make peace with your former spouse and the spouse's partner. Being a peacemaker—benefiting all bonds—means working deliberately to create peace with your adversaries. Even if you've been mistreated by an ex-spouse, even if he or she is still making trouble and creating difficulties, you can usually, over time, turn things around.

What to do with an ex-spouse who remains hostile

Both Rich and Karen live in the same town, with Karen having primary custody of their two children. Now Karen's new husband, Phil, has been offered a promotion if he transfers to a city several hours away. Against all appeals from Rich, Karen and Phil have decided to take the job and move. Rich is in total misery over the thought of living so far from his children.

What is Rich to do? In his case, he can't legally prevent the move. Rich's natural response to this crisis could be to hate Karen and Phil and try to ruin the relationship between the kids and their mother and stepfather.

As hard as it may be, Rich must rise above the circumstances and continue to be the greatest dad in the world and supportive of the other parents. Instead of following his natural inclinations to create misery for Karen or Phil, Rich must continue to benefit the bonds and connections between his children and their mother and stepfather. *More than anything*, Rich can achieve this by teaching his kids to remain loving and obedient to their mother and stepfather.

Making peace is far more important for his children than prevailing in custody battles. And peace is more important for the children than where they live. Rich's actions to accept and benefit the bonds will actually contribute toward a lifetime of stability and happiness for his children.

With his kids living hours away, Rich must continue to remain close to them. Distance and geography are not excuses for backing away. He's the dad and needs to continue acting as the dad. How can this be possible? Phone and email contact and making an effort to attend various school functions will be very important. The children will understand limited physical contact with their father but they won't understand lack of communication.

Rich will also want to give serious thought to moving to remain close to his children. Parents frequently write off this possibility without serious consideration. But, for the children's emotional stability, they need time with their father as much as they do with their mother and stepfather. We suggest that he make the move.

Giving your child the gift of their other parent

Jeff was only nine years old when his parents divorced and his dad left. Jeff remembers his dad moving into a new home with another woman and his mother having an extremely hard time emotionally. He remembers how angry he was and ready to blame his dad for everything and reject him completely.

Twenty years later, Jeff recalls clearly how his mother helped him over his anger and resentment so that he continued to care for his dad. She never allowed him to hate his father. She made him go see his dad, encouraged him to love his father and stepmother, and always supported his time with them.

Looking back, Jeff is extremely grateful to his mother for his strong relationship with his father. He realizes how close he was to full rejection of his father and stepmother.

Today Jeff will tell you *his mother gave him the gift of his father.*

Benefiting bonds means to begin to do something, anything, to build healthy relationships between your children and their other parent. Give your children the gift that will benefit them for a lifetime: the gift of their other parent and the parent's partner.

Whether you think the other parent and stepparent are right or wrong or good or bad, your relationship and your children's relationship with them are still critically important to the whole family's well-being. As long as your children remain protected and safe, the principle of being a benefit to all these relationships will promote the emotional health of your children.

To do good to an ex-spouse and that spouse's partner requires acting differently from how you may feel. You may even grieve and weep following your service of good. But your commitment must be to honor biological bonds, even if it causes you frustration.

The promise is clear: People who do what is right on behalf of their children, even though it may cause personal suffering, will end up with joy, reaping the enormous benefits of future family peace and emotionally healthy children.[3]

Examples of benefiting bonds

Sometimes people tell us that benefiting bonds and step-connections is simply beyond their ability. They can't even imagine doing such things! They are still focused on the past and the horrible actions carried out against them and their children.

We understand. We used to feel the same way ourselves.

Behaving kindly may seem just too difficult at first, but it gets easier with practice. And we assure you that benefiting all bonds and step-connections is critical if you are to have a healthy stepfamily.

Benefiting bonds means being flexible, accommodating, and easy to get along with. It means doing little things, special things, indicating that you are free from anger and destructive animosity.

Benefiting bonds is mainly absorbing the disturbing actions and words of other family members and not responding in kind. It means really disciplining *yourself* by mastering your emotions and words. At times benefiting bonds might mean it is better not to speak with former spouses or do them any favors because a cooling-off period may be best for all concerned.

Benefiting bonds may mean not going to court again, accepting some loss, because you know that any court action will only cause your children more emotional injury. It may mean returning to court to set proper standards because the other parent is completely out of control.

It may mean giving in and letting the other parent have more time with the children. It may mean paying more, serving more, driving more. Whatever you do, you do it not to "win," not to finally get your way, but because it is the best way to promote peace between families.

Paul the Apostle wrote, *Bless those who persecute you; bless and do not curse. Repay no one evil for evil. Have regard for good things in the sight of all men. If it is possible, as much as depends on you, live peaceably with all men.*[4]

If the other parent won't work toward peace, then you do it. It must be done.

What benefiting bonds is *not* is spending time at your former spouse's house helping with home maintenance. It's *not* spending extra time "just talking" with your ex over the phone. It's *not* sharing gifts during the Christmas season. It's *not* being extra friendly and overly sociable with your former spouse. Benefiting bonds does *not* mean trying to fulfill your emotional needs through your former spouse. Such actions create dependency and insecurity, alienate your present spouse, and do not benefit separate bonds.

Benefiting bonds is *not* a big fanfare. It's *not* about doing big things, making a big show.

Benefiting bonds is more about living your life and letting others live their lives without criticism or condemnation.

Here are some additional ways to benefit bonds:

- Get through all legal issues as quickly as possible. Wounds won't heal and nothing can be stabilized until legal matters are settled. Once legal decisions have been made, learn to accept them without bitterness.

- Litigation about finances and custody is an adult issue and has no place in determining a child's relationship with either parents or stepparents. *Children need to be with both parents.* Do not withhold your children because the other parent has not paid what is due you. Whether or not money has been exchanged does not even begin to compare with the importance of parent/child relationships and the support of nuclear bonds.

- See to it that your children's school has both parents' addresses and e-mails to receive school calendars, report cards, progress reports, and practice and game calendars. If your former spouse won't inform you of your children's schedules, take the initiative to learn about them yourself.

- When at a child's activity, invite the other parent to sit with you. Be the best "other" parent you can be. Welcome the other parent *and the parent's partner* into the lives of your children.

- Stepparents, encourage the parents to go to their children's practices and events without a word of discouragement. This is the life of the blending family—parents have to be with their children.

- When at an event that your ex-spouse is also attending, be positive when noticing your children's displays of affection toward their other parent and parent's partner. When visiting your child's classroom, enjoy the stories and drawings of both parents and partners.

- Never again be disrespectful toward your children's other parent or the other parent's partner.

- When celebrating holidays, birthdays, and other special occasions, try to emphasize the event and not the date of the event. Because of differing schedules in the separate households, an event frequently can't be celebrated on its particular day. Accept the fact that special events are sometimes celebrated on different days, ones that are more practical for each family.

- Don't be distraught if your adult children visit their other parent and not you over the holidays. Don't keep score. Let them feel absolutely free to choose wherever they want to go.

- Whenever speaking to the other parent or the other parent's partner, compliment them for what they have done for your child. It may be hard for you to do, but it will do wonders for creating peaceful relationships.

We're asking that you take serious steps to bring peace to each of your bonds and step-connections. A few moments of discomfort on your part when supporting and complimenting the other parents are insignificant in comparison with a lifetime of stability and emotional health for yourself and your children.

If you serve these bonds and connections, they'll serve you. Someone has to set the example and someone has to be the model. Are you up to it? Will you accept the challenge?

Jesus said, *"You have heard that it was said, 'You shall love your neighbor and hate your enemy.' But I say to you, love your enemies, bless those who curse you, do good to those who hate you, and pray for those who spitefully use you and persecute you, that you may be sons of your Father in heaven...."*[5]

This means to do it first. This means *you* set the standard and *you* become the model for right behavior.

Who are these people Jesus said we are to love? Our enemies, those who curse us, hate us, spitefully use us, and persecute us. What should be our response? We are to love, to bless, to do good, and to pray. For them! What a contrast.

The issue is not whether you or your children approve of the various bonds and connections in and around your family. The issue is how you respond to all these relationships.

When you do good to all of your nuclear bonds and step-connections, they will eventually become favorable toward you. And by your good works benefits will eventually return to you (we assure you, it does happen!).

Your kindness and willingness to serve will disarm others, be a calming agent to them, and create a measure of peace. You will discover that the other parent and stepparent won't fight with you. In fact, they may begin to return your kindness. But even if they don't, by benefiting bonds you will experience emotional relief and do much to insure the emotional health of your children.

~

Making Your Blending Family Work

Benefit all bonds and step-connections. By doing so, you and your children will be freed from anger and bitterness.

11

GOING THE DISTANCE WITH YOUR STEPCHILDREN
Benefiting All Inside Connections

Stepfamily connections largely determine blending family success. Blending families work largely because stepfamily connections work. They fail largely because stepfamily relationships fail.

Just because parents love their own children does not automatically qualify them to parent somebody else's children. Stepparents need training, lots of it, in the skills of stepparenting. Stepparents would do well to enter into their blending family with caution—as learners, not as trainers/teachers. Stepparents would do well to let the bio parent continue parenting while they take lots of time to let the stepparent/stepchild relationships slowly grow and gain momentum. Coming in like a locomotive, trying to make changes, demanding new behaviors and new rules only creates, not solves, problems.

Stepparents must *earn* parental rights. They must prove themselves worthy of respect and obedience. We agree that adults deserve a certain measure of respect simply because they're adults. But when stepparents cross the line and act as if they are automatically entitled to be parents, serious difficulties will begin to emerge. Stepparents will fare much better if they come into the family quietly, reverently, loaded with kindness, and light on discipline and judgment.

A stepdad benefiting a very resistant stepdaughter

Carole's mother and father divorced when she was nine years old. Following the divorce Carole's father abandoned the family. As a child, Carole faithfully expected her father to reappear any day. In fact, she would often fantasize about his return and what they would do together as father and daughter.

Carole's mother eventually remarried, which caused Carole great distress. She knew her mother wanted her to accept her stepdad, but she felt that if she did it might somehow prevent her father from returning home. So Carole maintained steady opposition to her stepdad throughout her teenage years.

When she turned nineteen, she fell in love with a man who asked her to move from California to the Midwest. Carole excitedly agreed. Even though both Carole's mother and stepdad were against the move, they couldn't stop her from going.

Upon learning that Carole intended to drive across the country to meet her boyfriend, the stepdad was greatly concerned. He told Carole that he would not allow her to make such a long trip alone. If she insisted on going, he would come along to make sure she arrived safely, then fly home.

When the day came for Carole to leave, there in the front passenger seat was her stepfather, and he adamantly refused to leave the car. He was going with her or she wasn't going at all.

Realizing finally that she could not change his mind, she determined to make the trip as miserable as possible. She refused to let him drive at all, wouldn't speak to him, and kept the radio at full volume. When they finally arrived, the stepfather told Carole that he loved her and then flew back to California.

Carole soon realized that she had made a big mistake—her boyfriend was alcoholic and abusive. The situation got so bad that one day she called home and her stepfather answered the phone. Hearing his kind voice, she began to cry. Without hesitation her stepdad told Carole that he would be right there. When he arrived, she was so overcome with relief that she threw her arms around him. They talked the whole way home, and this time, she let her stepdad drive.

Today, Carole will tell you that she loves this man as her own father and that he is the most wonderful man in the world.

Start quietly, go slowly

Awakened nuclear bonds will always reject non-biological adults who act as parents. Stepparents must seek to quiet these forces by supporting them. Carole eventually learned that her stepdad wasn't trying to replace her father. He only wanted Carole to know that he accepted her and wanted to be of benefit to her. This realization finally got through to Carole and quieted her bonds.

Stepparents do not win by force—they win by service. Time and time again, we have observed that when a stepparent enters into a family demanding immediate respect and obedience, the couple end up divorced and angry, and the stepparent is filled with bitter accusations against the parent and the stepchildren. The entire relationship was set up wrong, and no one knew how to handle the awakened nuclear bonds.

Jesus said, *"If anyone desires to come after Me, let him deny himself, and take up his cross, and follow Me. For whoever desires to save his life will lose it, but whoever loses his life for My sake will find it."*[1]

These verses are so important, telling stepparents how to have a great working family. If you try to rule—or over-rule—your family, you will probably lose your family.

Jesus also said, *"You know that the rulers of the Gentiles lord it over them, and those who are great exercise authority over them. Yet it shall not be so among you; but whoever desires to become great among you, let him be your servant."*[2]

Bill, a stepdad, attended a week-long summer camp with his stepson, Daniel Fisher. At the camp, everyone called him Mr.

Fisher, thinking that he was Daniel's father. Daniel wondered what his stepdad thought about being called Mr. Fisher. But Bill seemed not to mind and never corrected anyone—so Daniel didn't, either.

Going home in the car when the camp was over, Daniel asked Bill how he felt about being called Mr. Fisher. To his surprise, Bill told Daniel that he liked it. He considered it an honor to be thought of as Daniel's dad.

Daniel was deeply impressed and never forgot what Bill had said to him. He learned in the car that day how much his stepdad cared for him. Today Daniel still becomes emotional when he recalls the love of his stepfather and that conversation—a conversation that took place over thirty years ago.

Can you sense how quiet the nuclear bond must have been between the stepdad and this stepson? This is an example of a stepparent earning the right to be a stepparent.

Investments and benefits

One of the principles in the new universe of blending families is that stepparents are not *entitled* to but must *earn* a positive relationship with their stepchildren. And even then, the relationship will always remain conditional and tentative.

A good relationship between stepparents and stepchildren requires large investments of time, effort, and money by stepparents before they will ever enjoy a return. And sometimes stepparents may have to endure some pretty rocky situations before reaping any benefits. The reward from making such investments, though, will be a lifelong loving family.

Essie married Sudi, a woman with an 11-year-old daughter. Essie and the daughter got along famously. In fact their relationship was so good that when Essie and Sudi divorced, the daughter asked if she could continue living with her stepfather. Sudi quickly agreed, as she wanted her freedom and knew that Essie would provide a stable home for the girl.

When I heard this story from Essie, he was on his way to attend his stepdaughter's high school graduation. He mentioned to me that his stepdaughter was already enrolled in a four-year college, which he planned to finance.

Essie is one of the better examples of benefiting step-connections. He will reap wonderful rewards throughout his lifetime for his selfless commitment to his stepdaughter.

Good step-relationships can really benefit your marriage

Building relationships with stepchildren has an added bonus: Doing so will enhance the stepparent's relationship with the parent.

Because John had just gotten his driver's license, Roger, the stepdad, decided to take him out driving around the desert country. They took off for a three-day weekend, driving several hundred miles of highways, back roads, and freeways. Both the stepfather and stepson thoroughly enjoyed the trip.

When they returned home from their trip, and after observing her son's pleasure and excitement, the mom told her husband that she was grateful to him for spending the time with John. She said she would do anything for him and would never forget his kindness to her son. In fact, things went so well between Roger and the mom that he asked his stepson if there was anything else he could do for him!

Doing good for a stepchild is doing something equally good, if not more so, for the parent!

Making the benefits meaningful

Benefiting step-connections means doing things for your stepchildren that are *meaningful to them*. Start with small things.

- Help with homework, talk through problems, or go out for a pizza and soda.

- Redecorate your stepchild's bedroom. Can you help with repainting, new furniture, or a new wall hanging? Every stepparent will be pleased to have items in the stepchild's room that the child likes and *that are associated with the stepparent*.

- Take the kids boating or whitewater rafting. How about snow skiing or rock climbing? How about shopping or going to the library together?

- Travel with your stepkids. Can you arrange a short or lengthy trip? Plan to travel to see something of interest to them, maybe a national park or a water park.

- Treat your stepchildren with respect. When asking them to do something, say please and thank you.

- Never condemn or criticize their loyalty toward their other parent, even though that loyalty may appear in many forms in your family, even negative forms toward you.

- Be generous, with no strings attached. This is a critical component in winning your stepchildren's acceptance.

- Being a benefit to your stepchildren means spending time, effort, and money on them. You will be investing in future relationships by devoting yourself to a cause—the cause being the health of the kids in your blending family.

In your stepfamily there are no entitlements for stepparents—everything is earned. Once earned, you will reap a lifetime return of enjoyment and family happiness through your investment.

~

Making Your Blending Family Work

You earn a good relationship with your stepchildren through your words and actions.

12

ALLOWING CHILDREN ALONE TIME WITH THEIR OWN PARENT

Benefiting Inside Bonds Through Individual Attention

Married couples need time alone together. With all the demands of the bonds and step-connections in their blending families, time to be alone can easily get lost in the shuffle.

Children share in the same need to be alone with just their parents. They, too, have a desire for individual attention from both of their biological parents.

Illustrated below are a young girl and her two parents. Her parents are divorced and both are remarried. The two families together have seven nuclear bonds. The young girl also has two step-connections and two stepbrother and stepsister connections, for a total of eleven major bond/connections in and around her life. She is a small voice easy to be forgotten in the midst of a family filled with dominant and needy voices.

Figure 5

For her peace and stability, the young girl's bonds with her mom and dad must be recognized and strongly supported. These bonds cannot be ignored. In fact, the girl's emotional health depends upon reinforcing these two nuclear bonds. When parents divorce and form new families, the new marital bonds certainly need attention, but the children continue to require the same focus and support of both parents.

Time deprivation

Jackie and Kevin had five children in their blending family. With all the kids in elementary and junior high school, their blending family was a typical madhouse of sports practices, games, and various lessons. Time after school and weekends were filled with various kid activities.

But what Jackie and Kevin did not know or even think about was giving priority to spending individual time with each of their own children.

They didn't realize that it was because of this lack of individual attention their children were showing signs of feeling somewhat troubled and restless.

The nuclear bonds inside the children were awakening. They were starved due to lack of individual attention from their biological parents.

Jackie and Kevin's family was experiencing bond deprivation—meaning that individual nuclear bonds were suffering from time deprivation. Everyone was so busy with the family's activities that the individual needs of family members were being ignored.

Satisfied nuclear bonds accept the presence of non-biological family members in the home. Time deprived nuclear bonds create a non-welcoming atmosphere between step-connections. Suddenly non-biological family members appear as intruders into the family. With nuclear bond deprivation, the climate of the family changes from welcoming step-members to wanting some of them gone.

What was needed in this blending family was for bonded members to spend some individual time together—in other words, pay attention to the nuclear bonds.

Part of building a loving stepfamily means seeing to it that all bonded members have some time alone.

Kevin and Jackie didn't realize that unity in a blending family includes a measure of separation along bonded lines. The parents knew instinctively that *they* needed private time alone, but didn't translate this to the needs of their children. When one of the children tried to be alone with a biological parent, the stepparent always seemed to be around. The parents did not realize how their constant togetherness eventually became an irritant to the kids.

Because couples share the same biology, they enjoy being together much of the time. But this doesn't mean that the children will feel the same way. Parents tend to imagine that their children feel the same closeness to their spouses—the children's stepparents—as they do. Yet, unlike a married couple, there is no nuclear bond between stepchildren and stepparents. Instead of welcoming the presence of the stepparent, sometimes the children would like the stepparent to just go away.

Who would ever think that constant togetherness in a blending family might actually work against family unity and happiness?

Being able to breathe again

This new principle was like a breath of fresh air in Kevin and Jackie's family. Both Jackie and Kevin were relieved that they no longer had to feel guilty about wanting to be alone with their own kids, and refrained from criticizing each other for wanting the same thing.

Also, once the children had time alone with their biological bonds, they no longer viewed their stepparent as a competitor for their parent's time. And once the children felt that their parent was singularly committed to them, the nuclear bonds quieted down. The children were comforted in knowing that if they needed some individual time, they could get it.

The solution to the difficulty in Kevin and Jackie's blending family was to move from being totally "family-minded" to being *"bonded-minded."* They learned that each nuclear bond needed to be understood, identified, accepted, benefited, *and* given individual attention.

Couple suffocation

Jenetha and I discovered in our own blending family that it wasn't the kids who needed a breath of fresh air—it was *us!*

Because of work and our extremely busy family Jenetha and I were hardly ever alone. And when we finally were alone, we tried to cram together all of our necessary family discussions and our neglected emotional relationship into one meeting time. It just didn't work!

Our precious time together amounted to little more than a business meeting. Complicated discussions often ended in disagreements and strong emotions which destroyed any desire for romance and intimacy. It seemed best *not* to spend any time alone together because when we did, we came away unhappy.

In fact, our times alone together seemed to create more problems rather than solve them.

We realized that we had to make some changes. So what we did was limit our young children's schedules to one main extracurricular activity a year, try to limit overtime at work, and volunteer a bit less at church. We determined that we needed to have two uninterrupted times per week, alone.

Our first time together would be to take care of the business aspect of running our family. Our second time together would be for ourselves, to build our personal relationship, with no discussion of family affairs. We agreed that anything sensitive or difficult or that had to be hammered out would be talked about during our first meeting. The second time together would involve doing things that were fun and personal and strictly for our own enjoyment.

We realized that the words of King Solomon were extremely important to the personal health of our own marriage: *My beloved spoke, and said to me, 'Rise up, my love, my fair one, and come away. For, lo, the winter is past, the rain is over and gone. The flowers appear on the earth; the time of singing has come…Rise up, my love, my fair one, and come away!'*[1]

The importance of individual attention to emotional health

The Scriptures tell us that relationships between bonded members are critical. Great significance is placed on the relationships between spouses, and between parents and their children.

When bonds are in disconnect, people appear to be empty and under emotional stress.

In the Bible God said that it was the relationships between children and their fathers and fathers and their children that would determine whether He would judge, or not judge, mankind.[2]

Consider Joseph in Egypt, a prime minister endowed with majesty, power, and authority. He was surrounded by beauty and unimaginable wealth—yet he felt deep distress and dissatisfaction in being absent from his biological family.[3]

Consider Jacob and Esau, how after years of enmity and living far apart something was deeply resolved at their reunion.[4]

Then there's King David, who wept loudly over the death of his son, Absalom, the very person who became David's enemy, stole his kingdom, and defiled his wives.[5]

And don't the scriptures offer a magnificent promise that honoring bonded relationships will ensure a lifetime of emotional health and stability for children? The Bible says that if children honor and obey their father and mother, it will be well with them and they will live long on this earth.[6]

Making Your Blending Family Work

Making sure that bonded family members receive individual attention from their own parent will help keep the bonds quiet and accepting of step-members.

13

MAKING EVERY FAMILY MEMBER FEEL VALUED

Zero Neglect Toward Any Bond or Connection

Some of the greatest difficulties in blending families arise when some bonds are given too much attention, too much time, or too much energy, resulting in the *neglect* of other bonds and step-connections.

Concentrating on one bond *at the expense* of others is favoritism. If there isn't a good reason for the extra attention (something like a major illness), awarding one bond or step-connection more attention than another is lethal to blending families. Favoritism awakens jealousies and resentments that can dismantle the best of families.

Benefiting all stepfamily members through zero neglect means that no bond or step-connection is overlooked or disregarded. Zero neglect means that all of the blending family members experience a sense of well-being and feel reasonably satisfied.

Neglect occurs when individuals in the blending family perceive that they are receiving less favor, less time, and/or less material goods than other family members. Their sense of fairness is violated. They feel dishonored. They experience a sense of loss, which builds anger or resentment and sadness.

A bad day at a football game

Once when Jenetha and I attended a college football game, sitting right in front of us was a man, a woman, and a young boy. It became clear to us that this man and woman were on a date and had brought the woman's son along with them. The boy appeared to be the unhappiest kid on earth.

All during the football game the adults sat with their arms around each other, completely absorbed in each other, oblivious to the football game and the young boy. It was clearly apparent that the boy didn't have any interest in the game and was upset with his mother's attention to the man.

When the man left to purchase some food and returned with hot dogs and drinks, the boy put his head down and sobbed. From where I was sitting I could see tears rolling down the boy's arms. The hot dogs were covered in mustard, and evidently the boy hated mustard. For him this appeared to be the last straw. Not only did the man steal his mother, he also smothered his hot dog with mustard. The mother, seeing her son in such a pathetic condition, finally turned her attention from her partner to her son.

Now it was the man's turn to be upset. So here's the mother, sitting between two miserable people, trying to tend to both her partner and her son, and at the same time frantically wiping mustard off of the hotdog bun. The scene would have been comical if it weren't so sad.

What went wrong? The couple's *priorities*. They had expected the boy to be absorbed in the game so that they could focus on each other. Not only was their physical behavior highly inappropriate, they also didn't seem to care at all if the boy was miserable. They ignored him in order to benefit themselves. It was only when disaster struck that the mother forced herself to pull away from her partner and try to fix the problem with her son.

We suspected that this wasn't an isolated incident. The couple's priority was likely always on themselves, at the expense of this young boy.

Priority of bonds

One couple told us that the reason their blending family was so successful was that they were careful always to put their marriage first over the rest of their blending family.

Hardly ten minutes later, another couple told us that the success in their family was due to their always giving the kids first priority.

Because both stepfamilies were thriving, we knew the couples were essentially saying the same things. Both families would agree that, although they focused on certain relationships over others in their stepfamilies, still none of the other family members felt excluded or neglected.

We were happy to congratulate both couples and agree with them because it sounded as if *none of the other family members felt neglected.*

Here is the principle: Regardless of the priority of relationships, if family members never feel slighted, uncared for, or mistreated, things will be good for the stepfamily.

Destructive stepfamily models

Below are six blending family models. Each model is an example of ways to create non-working, unbalanced blending families:

Model 1: Believing that *your blending family* is more important than your children's other family. You wish that all of the former spouses and partners would just go away.

Model 2: Believing that *you as a couple are* more important than your children. You push your children to live with their other parents or outright ignore them, leaving them to manage on their own.

Model 3: Accepting *your spouse and your own children* but outright rejecting your spouse's children. You try to make your stepkids feel unwelcome so they will stay away.

Model 4: Believing that *your own children* are more important than your spouse. At times of conflict, you side with your children over your spouse. You spend most of your time apart from your spouse to be with your kids.

Model 5: Assigning a *higher priority to your children and stepchildren* than to yourselves. Your children are the lords and you, the parents, the servants. You and your spouse spoil your children to the neglect of your own marriage.

Model 6: Giving priority to your own self, making sure that your own personal needs and wants are satisfied to the neglect of everyone else.

What's the solution? The correct model is one in which no member of the family feels neglected. All family members feel satisfied and content.

The correct model is *behaving* as if every bond and every step-connection is equally important, regardless of your personal feelings or priorities.

Priorities will always ebb and flow, depending on the needs and quality of the relationships. But whatever relationship you privately prioritize, other family members should never know the difference. You should make sure that everyone in the family feels satisfied and content.

Insuring that no bond or step-connection feels slighted is critical in keeping nuclear bonds quiet. Any hint of neglect will cause trouble and awaken the powerful force of the nuclear bond.

Internal bank accounts

How can you keep track of the emotional health of each of your family members? What works well is if you think of each person in your family as an individual bank account. Each child and each adult in the family is an "account" that rises and falls based on the investment by you, the parents, in that account. If a person in your family feels lonely and left out, the account is down. If a family member feels included and of value, the account is up.

Parents in successful stepfamilies keep mental notes on how everyone is doing and whether the account of every family member is in good shape.

Investing in your children's bank accounts means giving time to the relationship, doing things together, working together, and building memories. It's being present at the kid's activities. It's talking about school, teachers, friends, and subjects of interest with the kids. It's having fun together, taking vacations to theme parks, or playing at the lake. It's working together to complete a homework project, shopping and purchasing household items or clothes, doing various garden or art projects together, helping to repair a vehicle, or doing various maintenance jobs together around the home. It means complimenting your child on a job well done.

Satisfaction and peace in a blending family depend on maintaining high reserves in everyone's account. As long as you and your spouse and your children have adequate reserves in your accounts, you will have a smoothly-running blending family.

Uneven playing fields

Sometimes the problem with priorities comes not so much from you or the stepparent as it does from grandparents or other parents or relatives.

In one blending family the mother's parents showered their biological grandchildren with nice clothes and expensive gifts but gave only token presents to the step-grandchildren, exhibiting great favoritism toward their own grandchildren over the other kids in the family.

So the mother quickly put her foot down. She told her parents that their gifts would not be welcome if they continued to be so partial in gift-giving. The mother then screened all of the children's gifts from the grandparents when they arrived at her home. The grandparents soon learned to comply with the mother's ultimatum.

But what are you to do when the other *parent* showers gifts on his or her children?

This was the case with a parent whose ex-husband had the means to give his kids expensive gifts and take them on exotic vacations and cruises. The parents of the stepbrothers and stepsisters were not able to provide equal gifts or vacations for their children.

In spite of the differences in gifts and vacations, the parents in the blending family still found ways to keep the children's emotional bank accounts full. In their home, they practiced equality among all of the children, and during holidays or for birthdays the parents gave the kids similar types of gifts.

The blending parents also fully endorsed the other parent taking his children on wonderful trips and giving them expensive gifts, and accepted the way things were. They encouraged the children to enjoy themselves on their travels and wanted them to freely share their experiences when they returned home.

The parents also trained the other stepbrothers and -sisters who were not able to travel to accept the situation as a part of life's realities. They taught them not to criticize or be envious of the opportunities available to their stepbrothers and step-sisters—lessons these kids will carry with them all their lives.

Most important for the children, the parents saw to it that each child found something in which to excel. Whether it was sports, academics, music, personality, friends, or school leadership, each child 'owned' something special and unique that no one else had, and therefore never felt jealous of or less important than the other kids in the family.

Benefiting your stepfamily means to level the playing field in your own home and honor every child equally so that no one feels slighted or left out. Whatever happens outside your family is beyond your control and therefore has to be accepted and embraced.

Making Your Blending Family Work

Regardless of the personal priorities of you or your spouse, no member of your blending family should feel slighted or neglected.

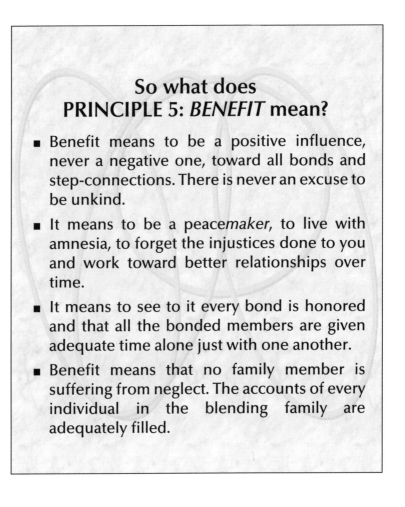

So what does
PRINCIPLE 5: *BENEFIT* mean?

- Benefit means to be a positive influence, never a negative one, toward all bonds and step-connections. There is never an excuse to be unkind.

- It means to be a peace*maker*, to live with amnesia, to forget the injustices done to you and work toward better relationships over time.

- It means to see to it every bond is honored and that all the bonded members are given adequate time alone just with one another.

- Benefit means that no family member is suffering from neglect. The accounts of every individual in the blending family are adequately filled.

14

LOVING YOUR STEPFAMILY

What Grace and Forgiveness Really Look Like

Applying the principles found in this book is essential to creating a great stepfamily. They are high-speed principles, meaning that if you act on them you will notice an almost immediate positive change in how your family operates. To the degree they are, or are not, put into practice is a reliable predictor of your family's potential for success or failure.

After reading about the five principles can you now understand and appreciate the importance of nuclear bonds and step-connections? Can you identify all of yours? Are you truly able to accept every one of them? Are you separated from all past relationships? Are you able to be of some benefit to your children's other parent and that parent's partner? Are you giving your spouse and kids individual attention? Does everyone in your family feel valued? Does any nuclear bond or step-connection feel neglected?

If you follow the principles we have described, the bonds and connections under your control should remain quiet and satisfied. The solution is to begin *now* to get on the path to a peaceful and stable future. It takes time to build habits of acceptance, separation, and benefit. But through practice and perseverance you *can!*

A woman who was struggling with a recent divorce told us that the principles we were sharing were a bit too idealistic for her. She said that to identify all bonds, accept, and benefit them would be not only very difficult but practically impossible for her to do. She was just too hurt and angry with her ex-spouse to implement the principles.

The woman appeared to me to be reasonable and responsible. My answer to her was that in the future, perhaps years in the future, she would probably recover from her current emotional heaviness, that she would most likely remarry, and that the relationship between her former husband and herself would stabilize. I also said when this all happened, she would then probably be willing to practice the principles.

And she agreed.

But I told her that by the time she feels recovered and is ready to implement the principles, her children will have suffered terrible emotional damage. How will she feel then, knowing that she could have prevented much of their injury?

This woman does not have the luxury of waiting until everything settles down in her life before bringing health to her kids. Waiting until *she's* ready to incorporate the principles will emotionally stunt her children. For years to come she will sadly watch her grown children fail in an adult world because she was unwilling to act.

The woman must force herself and her children to behave responsibly in their present difficult environment. She has to prevent herself and her children from retreating into the damaging mind-set of self-pity, personal entitlement, accusation, and blame.

They say that time heals all wounds. But waiting for the right time in the future, until you are emotionally healed to begin incorporating these principles is a mistake. You must act now for the sake of your children and their future.

Whether you feel like it or not, it is time to take control of your circumstances. Bring these principles into your life and into the lives of all your family members now! *Your* emotional health and *your kids'* emotional health are on the line.

Grace and forgiveness

Throughout the entire book we have not mentioned the words "grace" or "forgiveness"—words that are commonly used in literature for stepfamilies, particularly when discussing the difficult aspects of human relationships. Yet, in our book the words are uncommonly absent.

But, in another sense, the entire book is about grace and forgiveness.

The question is, when you ask God for His grace and forgiveness, what does it look like? And, when *you* seek to show grace and forgiveness, what do you do?

God's grace and forgiveness to you are found in these five principles. And the grace and forgiveness you show to your stepfamily and those outside your stepfamily are the principles in action.

What is God's grace and forgiveness? It is understanding the critical design of nuclear bonds. It is identifying and accepting all bonds and step-connections. It is separating and not interfering with outside family members. It is benefiting all bonds and connections, allowing your partner without complaint to give individual attention to his or her own children. It is seeing to it that no bond or connection under your authority is neglected.

Receiving grace and forgiveness comes before giving them. By humbly asking God for His grace and forgiveness, you will not only receive His gifts but will be empowered to fully grant grace and forgiveness to others.[1]

Once you put all the principles into practice, you and your partner can be assured that you are exercising gracious and forgiving behavior, that grace and forgiveness are working well in your family.

Fulfilling these five principles is fulfilling God's grace and forgiveness. It's what will keep your family stable and peaceful in the midst of complex relationships. It means that your own sense of stability and peace will overflow to your children and to your children's other family members.

Putting grace and forgiveness into practice may be difficult, particularly at first. But you will discover that the benefits so far outweigh the difficulties that your hard work will be well worth it.

You cannot receive God's grace and forgiveness, nor will you be able to give God's grace and forgiveness in the form of these five principles, if you continue to carry an attitude of non-forgiveness and harbor anger against others. Continuing to replay all of your disappointments and bad feelings will fill you with vengeance and hatred and animosity—emotions you are not designed to carry. The Scriptures say, *for the wrath of man does not produce the righteousness of God.*[2] This means that holding on to anger will never bring happiness to your family. Righteousness can never come out of wrath.

Our challenge to every reader is to follow after God's righteousness by living the five principles outlined in this book. Receive God's grace and forgiveness. Be a person of grace and forgiveness.

Jesus said, *You have heard that it was said, 'You shall love your neighbor and hate your enemy.' But I say to you, love your enemies, bless those who curse you, do good to those who hate you, and pray for those who spitefully use you and persecute you, that you may be sons of your Father in heaven....*[3]

What is Jesus saying? He is saying to love, bless, do good, and pray for those who spitefully use you—and to do it *now!*

~

Making Your Blending Family Work

To model God's grace and forgiveness is to embrace the five principles.

Following after God's grace and forgiveness is the only way your blending family will ever find peace and contentment.

APPENDIX

End Notes

Preface

[1] Dr. E. Mavis Hetherington, principle researcher of the "Virginia Longitudinal Study of Divorce and Remarriage" (the most comprehensive study of divorce and remarriage in America) and author of the book, *For Better or for Worse,* confirmed that *the overall divorce rate for stepcouples is between 65% and 70%.* This finding comes from the study but was not specifically reported in Dr. Hetherington's published research. Furthermore, because not all stepfamilies have the same level of complexity, Dr. Hetherington went on to specify that in "simple stepfamilies" (where only one partner brings a child or children to the new marriage) the divorce rate is 65 percent; when both partners have children from previous relationships ("complex stepfamilies"), the divorce rate is slightly more than 70 percent.

In the research study: "Cohabitation, Marriage, Divorce, and Remarriage," by the United States National Center for Health Statistics (Vital Health Stat 23-22), 2002, by Bramlett, MD and Mosher, WD, 39 percent of remarried couples divorced within 10 years. This study does not contradict Dr. Hetherington's research, which seems to suggest that divorce increases 26% to 31% following the ten year mark. This suggestion appears likely as the graph shows that divorce increases dramatically with the years. Please see www.cdc.gov/nchs/data/series/sr_23/sr_23_022.pdf, page 24, figure 38: Probability that the second marriage breaks up by duration of marriage and race/ethnicity: United States, 1995. If the website cannot be accessed, please go to http://www.cdc.gov/nchs/mardiv.htm. On the left menu touch Vital Statistics, then click on Marriages and Divorces. Scroll down to Other Sources of Marriage and Divorce Statistics and click on Cohabitation, Marriage, Divorce, and Remarriage in the United States. Under the heading, "Cohabitation, Marriage, Divorce, and Remarriage in the United States. Series Report 23, Number 22. 103pp.," click on View/download PDF.

Introduction: Stepfamilies are Nothing Like First Marriages

[1] Genesis 1:1

Chapter 1: The Most Powerful Bonds in the World— The Bonds Between Husband and Wife and Parent and Child

[1] Even though an adoption isn't a biological connection, the connection can be so close that it appears to be the exact duplicate of a nuclear bond. Because there is so much similarity, in fact, we call the connection an *Adoption Bond.*

Chapter 3: Identifying the Critical Relationships in Your New Family

[1] When determining the number of connections among stepbrothers and stepsisters, two or more children of the same biology are counted as one individual.

Remember not to count Couple 1's children as step-brothers to Tina's other biological children. They are half-brothers.

Chapter 4: Accepting Your Children's Other Parent into Their Lives

[1] 1 Peter 3:8b-11

Chapter 7: The Authority of the Biological Parent in Discipline

[1] Luke 16:1-13

Chapter 9: Giving Freedom to the Parent/Child Relationship

[1] The key to the daughters' getting along with their father and with Kathy, at this moment, is the mother. We haven't discussed Al's or Kathy's response to the mother, which is a critical component in bringing about peace between opposing former family members. On this subject we shall remain silent, as the focus of this chapter, separating bonds, is on how Kathy should respond to the problems with Al and his children.

Chapter 10: *Making* Peace with Your Ex and Your Ex's Partner

[1] Matthew 5:9

[2] Proverbs 15:1

[3] Psalms 126:5,6: *Those who sow in tears shall reap in joy. He who continually goes forth weeping, bearing seed for sowing, shall doubtless come again with rejoicing, bringing his sheaves with him.*

[4] Romans 12:14,17,18

[5] Matthew 5:43-45a

Chapter 11: Going the Distance with Your Stepchildren

[1] Matthew 16:24-25

[2] Matthew 20:25b-26

Chapter 12: Allowing Children Alone Time with Their Own Parent

[1] Song of Solomon 2:10-12a, 13b

[2] *Behold, I will send you Elijah the prophet before the coming of the great and dreadful day of the LORD. And he will turn the hearts of the fathers to the children, and the hearts of the children to their fathers, lest I come and strike the earth with a curse.* Malachi 4:5-6

[3] Genesis 45:1-2; 46:29

[4] Genesis 33:4

[5] 2 Samuel 18:33

[6] Ephesians 6:1-3

Chapter 14: Loving Your Stepfamily

[1] Accepting grace and forgiveness is accepting God's Person of grace and forgiveness into your life. We first acknowledge our shortcomings and need of a Savior. We then pray to God confessing our sins and believing in Jesus Christ as our personal Lord and Savior. Through Him we receive grace and forgiveness from God.

Romans 3:23: *for all have sinned and fall short of the glory of God.*

1 John 1:9: *If we confess our sins, He is faithful and just to forgive us our sins and to cleanse us from all unrighteousness.*

Romans 10:9,10: *that if you confess with your mouth the Lord Jesus and believe in your heart that God has raised Him from the dead, you will be saved. For with the heart one believes unto righteousness, and with the mouth confession is made unto salvation.*

John 1:17 *For the law was given through Moses, but grace and truth came through Jesus Christ.*

See Matthew 18:21-35 regarding receiving God's grace and forgiveness and the obligation to show the same grace and forgiveness to others.

[2] James 1:20

[3] Matthew 5:43-45a

A Guide for Group Study:
Questions for Thought and Discussion

Introduction: Stepfamilies are Nothing Like First Marriages

Summary: *Through wisdom a house is built, and by understanding it is established; by knowledge the rooms are filled with all precious and pleasant riches.*

1. What were your expectations when you started your blending family? How is your family different from what you thought it would be?

2. Can you identify with the dad in the Home Depot story trying to please everyone and yet feeling as if everything he does is wrong? What have been some of your experiences?

3. What are some of the circumstances in your family that you would identify as second-universe issues (issues that would never come up in a first marriage)?

Principle 1: Understand

Chapter 1: The Most Powerful Bonds in the World— The Bonds Between Husband and Wife and Parent and Child

Summary: Nuclear bonds are the absolute seat of emotional health through which children and parents can develop stable, happy lives.

1. Describe your understanding of what the nuclear bond is, and its importance.

2. Describe your relationship with your parents when you were a child. What made it good or bad? Talk about your current relationship with your parents.

3. How did reading about nuclear bonds change your perception of your childhood relationship with your parents? How did it change your perception of your relationship with your children and/or stepchildren?

Chapter 2: Why Merging Two Families So Often Fails

Summary: Awakened nuclear bonds unify biological members against outsiders. Learning to quiet them is key to achieving a peaceful and successful blending family.

1. What was your relationship with your future stepchildren before you married? How has it changed since you married?

2. How do the loyalties of the nuclear bond affect you and your blending family? How do they affect your children with their other family?

3. How hard has it been in your family to overlap bonds with the stepparent and stepchildren? What kind of problems have you or your children had?

Principle 2: Identify

Chapter 3: Identifying the Critical Relationships in Your New Family

Summary: Your family is defined today by the people who are part of your blending and extended family. Identification of every bond and step-connection is critical to making your blending family work.

1. Explain why identifying bonds and connections is important.

2. Was it difficult for you to acknowledge the nuclear bonds and step-connections in your blending family? Why? Were there some members you wanted to leave out?

3. When you made your family diagram, how many biological bonds did you find in your family? How many step-connections?

4. Evaluate the condition of each of your bonds and step-connections. Which bonds or connections are doing well? Which ones are in trouble?

Principle 3: Accept

Chapter 4: Accepting Your Children's Other Parent into Their Lives

Summary: Accept all bonds and step-connections. *"God has called us to peace."*

1. What type of relationship do you have with your ex-spouse?

2. Even though you may not approve of your child's other parent, do you recognize the importance of your child's nuclear bond with that parent? Why is it important to accept the other parent? (Acceptance does not mean to expose your children to any real endangerment.)

3. Blending families must develop amnesia about the past. Are there some incidents you need to forget about? What can you do to help yourself accept what has happened?

Chapter 5: Accepting Your Spouse's Children into Your Life

Summary: Accepting nuclear bonds and step-connections inside your family means to see to it that all family members are respected.

1. Why is it important to accept and not undermine your spouse's bond with his or her children?

2. Talk about any of the nuclear bonds in your family you have trouble accepting.

3. How can you continue to support the bond between the parent and child if you are the one being rejected?

Chapter 6: The True Role of the Stepparent

Summary: Parents bear the responsibility for their own children, not stepparents. The stepparent should receive thanks and recognition from the parent for any service or kindness to the parent's children. Stepparents must show acts of kindness and care to all stepchildren.

1. What role in your child's life do you expect the stepparent to take? In what role as the biological parent do you see yourself?

2. Discuss what the "grandparent concept" means. How can this work in your blending family?

3. If you have expected your spouse to share in all your parenting obligations, what adjustments can you make to reduce the obligations?

4. Make a plan together of how you will work to change your behavior, change responsibility toward various household jobs, and change expectations of each other.

Chapter 7: The Authority of the Biological Parent in Discipline

Summary: Five responses by stepparents to parents who *will not* discipline their kids and prevent you from making corrections:

(1) Let the small stuff go.

(2) Find a third party arbitrator.

(3) Understand that part of parenting may be allowing a child to experience failure.

(4) If your spouse's kids are having a negative influence on your children, lay down separate rules.

(5) If a situation becomes truly harmful or threatening, remove yourself and your children.

1. How is discipline handled in your household? How is it working? If it is not working, what is your next step?

2. What good can come from a child experiencing failure? How can you as a stepparent remain supportive?

3. The idea of separate rules for kids often surprises adults in blending families. How could separate rules ease tensions in your family?

Principle 4: Separate

Chapter 8: Letting Your Ex Live His (Her) Own Life

Summary: When adults separate from outside bonds and step-connections, families can experience peace.

1. Talk about the outside bonds in your stepfamily. Which bonds have been awakened? What can you do to quiet them?

2. How involved are you in your ex's life?

3. What happens when you attempt to control how your ex cares for your child? Does the other parent do the same to you? What happens then?

Chapter 9: Giving Freedom to the Parent/Child Relationship

Summary: At times, stepparents may need to retreat and let parents rebuild a relationship with their own children.

1. Is there a child in your family who is rejecting the parent and/or stepparent? How is this affecting your marriage?

2. What does giving your spouse the freedom to rebuild the relationship with his or her own child mean to you? How can you put this into practice?

Principle 5: Benefit

Chapter 10: *Making* Peace with Your Ex and Your Ex's Partner

Summary: Benefit all bonds and step-connections. By doing so, you and your children will be freed from anger and bitterness.

1. What is your reaction to the principle of benefiting all bonds?

2. Our natural instincts are to fight fire with fire. Discuss how this philosophy may have hurt your children.

3. Are you ready to be a peace*maker*? Name something, no matter how small, that you can do today to benefit the other parent and the other parent's partner.

4. Discuss how benefiting all bonds can help your children. Even though difficult, how can you now benefit all bonds? What will you do and how will you do it?

5. Showing kindness to those who have hurt you can ultimately free you from negative emotions. Share a time when you did this and how it affected you.

Chapter 11: Going the Distance with Your Stepchildren

Summary: You *earn* a good relationship with your stepchildren through your words and actions.

1. What have you done to earn your current relationship with your stepchildren? Knowing what you know now, what will you do to improve the relationship?

2. Investing in your stepchildren may not reap rewards for years. What can you do as a couple to support each other during times when the stepchildren seem thankless and unappreciative of your efforts?

Chapter 12: Allowing Children Alone Time with Their Own Parent

Summary: Making sure that bonded family members receive individual attention from their own parent will help keep the bonds quiet and accepting of step-members.

1. Which of your family members, if any, feel left out and deprived? What can you do about it?

2. Building unity in blending families means that biologically-related family members are allowed to spend time apart from others in the family. Is this happening in your family? Talk about the value of individual attention between parent and child.

3. Talk about your family's typical schedule. Where can you carve out time just for you and your kids and just for you and your spouse?

Chapter 13: Making Every Family Member Feel Valued

Summary: Regardless of the personal priorities of you or your spouse, no member of your blending family should feel slighted or neglected.

1. Can you identify your family in any of the six models? Knowing what you know now, what actions can you take to prevent neglect or emotional injury to any of your family members?

2. Discuss the current status of the emotional bank accounts of your children and step-children. Do you think every account is satisfied? How about the accounts of you and your spouse?

3. What can you do to insure that all bank accounts are full and satisfied?

Chapter 14: Loving Your Stepfamily

Summary: To model God's grace and forgiveness is to embrace the five principles. Following after God's grace and forgiveness is the only way your blending family will ever find peace and contentment.

1. At what point in your life did you ask God for His grace and forgiveness?

2. When will you be willing to take control of your circumstances and be the peacemaker with *all* of your family members?

3. Discuss the idea that doing the hard things now will free you from years of regret later.

4. Review and discuss the five principles in this book: Understand, Identify, Accept, Separate, and Benefit. With which ones have you had the most success? Which ones have been the most difficult for you? Are there any you are still struggling with? What new ideas have come to you?

INDEX

A

Abusive environments
defining 94

Acceptance vs. approval 40

Accepting
a troubled stepchild 53
inside connections 49
outside bonds and
connections 39
the disciplining process 68
the stepparent as a
stepparent 58
your adult stepchildren 55
your children's other parent
into their lives 39
your own kids 50
your spouse's children into
your life 49
your stepchildren 52

Acquisition vs. merger 56

Amnesia, a critical element of
success 44

Authority
parent 54

B

Bank accounts, internal 139

Benefiting
bonds 115
examples of 113
inside bonds through

individual attention 127
inside connections 119
outside bonds and
connections 107

Benefits
making them meaningful
125

Blending family
road to peace for everyone
22

Bonds
see Nuclear bonds

Boundaries
maintaining 93

C

Complex family system 11

Connections
see Step-connections

Couple suffocation 131

D

Dating a parent 3

Discipline
authority of the biological
parent in 68
solutions that work 71
1. Don't sweat the small
stuff 72
2. Consult a third party 75
3. Let the child fail 76

4. Separate rules 78
5. Separate from harmful
   stepchildren 80

E

Emotional health
   importance of attention to
   132

Expectations, unrealistic 60

Ex-spouse
   what to do when one
   remains hostile 110

F

Family system
   complex 11
   simple 11

Favoritism 140, 141

First universe
   the world of the first
   marriage 2

First-marriage bond 12

Forgiveness 143, 145

G

Gift of the other parent 112

Grace 143, 145

Grandparents
   the model for great
   stepparenting 61

H

Humility
   the power of 102

I

Identifying
   all nuclear bonds 27, 28
   critical relationships in your
   new family 27
   step-connections 31

Individual attention
   bio-children with parents
   127

Immorality 45

Investments and benefits 123

Involvement, lack of
   and lack of awareness 90

Irresponsibility 45

L

Loyalties 15

M

Making peace 108
   with your ex and your ex's
   partner 107

Married couples
   as a team 101
   time alone 127

Merger vs. acquisition 56

N

Neglect
  toward any bond or
    connection 134

Nuclear bonds 11, 15, 51
  awakened 22, 122
  between married couples 12
  between parents and
    children 12
  creation of 12
  demand for independence
    by 18
  failure to respect 41
  in first marriages 12
  loyalty of 15
  nuclear war 97
  overlapping of 19
  power of 14
  priority of 13,136
  problems with joining 18
  quieting 22, 123
  separating from all outside
    87
  separating from inside 96
  war 97
  why they work in some
    relationships and not in
    others 22

O

Overlapping of bonds 19

P

Parent authority 54

Parent/child relationship
  giving freedom to 96

Parental rights
  stepparents, earning 120

Parents and stepparents
  an important difference
    between 73

Playing field
  level 141
  uneven 140

Principle 1: Understand 9, 24

Principle 2: Identify 25, 36

Principle 3: Accept 37, 83

Principle 4: Separate 85, 104

Principle 5: Benefit 105, 142

Priorities
  of bonds 136
  uneven in stepfamilies 140,
    141

Protecting your kids 94

Q

Quieting bonds 22, 123

R

Rejection
  among stepfamily members
    49

Replace
  the biological parent 42

S

Second universe 7
can work 7
world of the stepfamily 2, 3

Separating from
an unsafe household 80
inside connections 96
outside bonds and
connections 87

Separation, successful
of yourself, not your kids 92

Simple family system 11

Standard stages of life 2

Stepchildren
acts of kindness toward all
65

Stepchildren, your
going slowly 122
going the distance with 119

Step-connection relationships
58

Step-connections
definition of 29
identifying 29, 31

Stepfamilies
appear identical to nuclear
families 1
live in another universe 2
why they have difficulties 20

Stepfamily connections
blending family success 119

Stepfamily models
destructive 137

Stepfamily, loving your 143

Stepparent
sustaining the 64
true role of the, 58
unrealistic expectations 60

Stepparents
not entitled 123
prisoners in their own
homes 69

Step-relationships, good
in a marriage 124

T

Time deprivation 128

U

Unconditional love 102

Understand
the climate of your family 80

Universe
first 2
second 2

Unrealistic expectations
of stepparents 80

Z

Zero neglect 135
toward any bond or
connection 134

About the Authors

Dr. Donald Partridge and his wife Jenetha are the proud parents/stepparents of a highly successful blending stepfamily of seven children. When Don and Jenetha met and married, they were both single parents—Don with two children and Jenetha with three. When they then added two of their own, their blending family became truly "yours, mine, and ours." As a result of interacting with other single parents and stepfamilies, Don and Jenetha came to realize that their personal experiences and difficulties were anything but uncommon. So in 1989 they committed their future life's work to providing knowledgeable, well-researched, practical solutions for single parents and stepfamilies.

Dr. Partridge earned his Bachelor of Arts degree at Patten College, his Master's in Theology degree at Fuller Seminary, and his Doctor of Philosophy degree at Oxford Graduate

School, with a focus on issues in remarriage. Don graduated summa cum laude and was valedictorian at Patten College and valedictorian at Oxford. He also received Oxford's Challis Award for doctoral work most likely to benefit Christianity. Don is a standing member of Oxford's Society of Scholars.

Jenetha is a registered nurse and consultant for a national home health and hospice company.

Together, Don and Jenetha are currently conducting conferences and workshops throughout the country. They are the founders and directors of the Institute for Family Research and Education, a non-profit corporation dedicated to providing quality educational assistance to single parents and stepfamilies.

IMAGINE THIS BOOK PRESENTED LIVE!

Authors Dr. Donald Partridge and Jenetha Partridge, nationally known speakers, look forward to addressing your group or audience.

Observe for yourself lives changed, families transformed, marriages saved, and children stabilized and on their way to emotional health.

"These guys are good!"

"I realize I've been damaging my children. I'm going to stop immediately."

"I finally know what to do and am at last moving in the right direction."

"I now have hope for my family."

"I can make these changes right now."

"If we had known this information before, we probably would not have broken up our blended family."

"I've been to many programs and workshops—but this one was the best!"

For more information please go to <u>www.blendingfamily.com</u>, or call 925-351-7000.

Give the gift of *Loving Your Stepfamily: The Art of Making Your Blending Family Work* to your relatives, friends, and colleagues

Order Here

Website: www.blendingfamily.com
Fax orders: 925-461-3472. Send this form.
Telephone: Call 925-351-7000. Have your credit card ready.

Postal Orders: The Institute for Family Research and Education, P.O. Box 10092, Pleasanton, CA 94588-0092

☐ **Yes**, I want _____ copies of *Loving Your Stepfamily: The Art of Making Your Blending Family Work* @ 14.95 each.

☐ **Yes**, I am interested in having Dr. Don and Jenetha Partridge conduct a seminar or workshop for my company, association, school, or church. Please send me information.

Name: _____

Organization: _____

Address: _____

City/State/Zip: _____

Email: _____ Phone (____)_____

QTY.	PRICE EACH	TOTAL
	$14.95	
Sales Tax: For California only, please add 8.75%		
Shipping: Please add $3.00 for one book, $1.00 for each additional book		

My check or money order for $_____ is enclosed.
Please make your check payable to IFRE.

Or, charge my ☐ Visa ☐ MasterCard

Card No.: _____

Exp. Date: _____ Signature: _____

ATTENTION: CHURCHES, CORPORATIONS, UNIVERSITIES, COLLEGES, AND PROFESSIONAL ORGANIZATIONS.

Discounts are available for quantity purchases of this book as gifts, for educational purposes, or as premiums for increasing magazine subscriptions or renewals. The use of particular book excerpts is allowed for specific needs, with permission of the publisher. For more information, please go to www.blendingfamily.com, or call 925-351-7000.